a.m.
9/93

D0392072

DATE DUE

AG 12 '88			
SE 10 '93			
SE 22 '95			
AG 1 '96			
NY 7 '01			
AP '05			

FE '86

DEMCO

TRAVELING
LIGHT

TRAVELING LIGHT

Every Woman's Guide to Getting There in Style

Leah Feldon

Drawings by Eduard Erlikh

G. P. PUTNAM'S SONS / NEW YORK

G. P. Putnam's Sons
Publishers Since 1838
200 Madison Avenue
New York, NY 10016

The Anti-Jet-Lag Diet was provided by Argonne National
Laboratory, 9700 South Cass Avenue, Argonne, IL 60439. In
order to receive an Anti-Jet-Lag Diet card, please write to the
Argonne National Laboratory at the above address and include a
stamped, self-addressed envelope.

Library of Congress Cataloging in Publication Data

Feldon, Leah, date.
  Traveling light.

  1. Travel.   2. Clothing and dress.   I. Title.
G151.F45   1985   910'.2'02   84-24187
ISBN 0-399-13042-X

Printed in the United States of America
1 2 3 4 5 6 7 8 9 10

Designed by Giorgetta Bell McRee

This one for Dad with love.

Acknowledgments

My sincere thanks to all those who have contributed their knowledge, personal experiences, ideas, insights, and inspirations: my parents, Paul and Henrietta Kahan; Connie Clausen and her associate Guy Kettelhack; Nancy Perlman; Diane Reverand; my great pal and fitness guru, Alison Pearl, especially for contributing the fine airplane exercises on pages 123–124; Joan Sibley; Eduard Erlikh; Lans Stout; David Baurac of the Argonne National Laboratory; world-class traveler Mary Pierson; David Kaufmann; and last but definitely not least, my superb right-hand woman, Melissa Pierson, without whose skills and dedication *Traveling Light* could not have been completed.

Contents

TRAVELING LIGHT

Introduction

We women have come a long way to reach the kind of freedom we enjoy in the eighties, and our traveling habits readily reflect that freedom. More women are traveling now than ever before. Traveling's so easy today that we hardly think twice about grabbing our gear, hopping into a car—or onto a bus, train, or plane—and taking off for parts unknown. More and more businesswomen are on the run too, and they must pick up and go sometimes with hardly a moment's thought.

But thinking twice—or even three times—could be the difference between a good trip and a great one. Thinking about what our perfect trip should include (for business or pleasure), and what to do or take along to make sure our trip is everything we want it to be is exactly the ticket.

In the old days, the problem of *what* to take was solved by simply taking everything—and then some. You might remember your mother getting ready for a trip by dragging out the three- or four-piece matched luggage set—complete with cosmetics case and suitcases large enough to handle a trip around the world in eighty days. The bags weighed a ton, of course, but a woman could always get her husband or a porter to do the carrying. So it really didn't matter if three blouses, two dresses, or a couple of pairs of shoes were never worn.

Today, though, we're heading out to places where they've never even heard of porters, or if they have, you can bet your bottom dollar they won't be there when you need them. And many more of us are traveling alone, without husbands or pack mules to bear our luggage burdens for us. Times have indeed changed!

These days, whether you're traveling for business or for pleasure, you want and *need* to be independent, to move quickly and know you won't have to worry endlessly about details. And you want the peace of mind that comes with knowing that you've got just the right clothing and accessories for all your needs—and that they won't weigh you down.

That's what *Traveling Light* is all about. Traveling light both in weight and in spirit. Knowing the tricks and shortcuts that help you take it easy and let the spontaneous joy of taking a trip have free play—but with all the advantages of careful planning and forethought.

Organization and style are obviously the keys to traveling light. It's a wonderful feeling to know you'll look great
wherever, and however, you go—to make an impression
on a client or your hosts, or just to be at ease with
yourself. But that confidence is tough to come by unless
you've brought the right things, and in the chapters to
come I'll tell you how to be sure. I'll bring up *everything*
you need to think about before you go, so you'll never
have to think about it once you're on the road. You'll be
surprised at how easy it is! The one surprise you'll never
have again, though, is that sinking feeling when you realize that, in all three pieces of luggage, *nothing* you've
packed goes together or looks right.

During my days as a fashion stylist, I did a lot of
location shooting, for both TV commercials and print
advertising. That meant, among other things, that I had to
be sure I had brought along just the right clothes and
accessories for each individual photograph or scene, and
in the perfect size to fit each individual model. Since we
often filmed in remote places where last-minute shopping
was impossible, I had no room for error. For the sake of
survival (not to mention my job) I became an expert in
the fine art of pre-trip planning and preparation. And so
can you.

There are three major areas of organization you need
to consider when preparing for a trip: your actual travel
arrangements, your wardrobe, and your personal appearance and needs. I'll give you tips on all three in the
chapters that follow. You'll get the benefit of my own
experience, and of all the experts I've consulted—travel

agents, luggage salesmen and representatives, business travelers, and "just plain folks." I've listened to people's complaints and most frequent problems, and I've provided the best solutions in these pages. The only thing I've left for you to figure out is where you want to go—and I've even included a few ideas on that!

The annotated lists at the back of the book are, like the other lists here, guidelines for you to follow. If there are some items listed that you don't normally use or wouldn't feel comfortable wearing, leave them out or make your own substitutions. The only point I want to make is that you *can* pare down to essentials and still travel in style and comfort.

Ready? Let's go!

1 On Your Mark, Get Ready, Organize

SETTING YOUR SCENE

The first decision of all, of course, is where to go. If you're gearing up for a business trip, your destination will be predetermined. Even so, there may be travel arrangements you'll need, or want, to make yourself. And those arrangements will affect what and how you pack.

If you're planning a vacation trip, you've got an infinity of options—all of which will influence your style of travel, means of transportation, quantity and kind of wardrobe, and so on.

I can't help you decide what sort of vacation you want (although a glance at the Temperature-Climate Guide on pages 89–93 may help, as will conversations with a good travel agent and with friends who have tastes and interests similar to your own). But I can give you a few tips, to make trip planning easier on yourself. There are basically two ways you can go: self-planning—relying on guidebooks and making reservations for yourself—and using a travel agent to make most plans for you. Whichever you choose, your itinerary is usually your own, and takes some forethought.

Travel agents. For many people, travel agents are the only way to go. Their access to computers makes it easy for them to see at a glance the best or cheapest way to travel, and they can make up a ticket for you on the spot.

It's important to find an agent who is willing not only to listen to you, but to spend time on research as well. If your idea of a great vacation is a deserted beach in Tahiti, it can be more than disconcerting to find yourself booked for a stay in a crowded tourist resort instead.

But don't worry—there are plenty of good travel agents around. So if you suspect an agent is trying to book you quickly and get you out of the office, find another. It's a good idea to check to see that your agent is "C.T.C."—a Certified Travel Consultant, and/or a member of ASTA (American Society of Travel Agents). When you find an agent you like, go back to him/her for subsequent travel arrangements: Your agent will come to know you and your preferences, making future trips even easier.

Travel agents also have information about insurance you might need on your trip, inoculation requirements for foreign countries, currency and customs restrictions, and a host of details that can plague the unwary traveler. They can also act as a liaison between you and the carrier, which is especially important if you're going on a cruise or by charter. Since their services are almost always free to the traveler, travel agents provide one of the best deals around, and they can be crucial for peace of mind about an upcoming trip.

Travel literature. If you want to plan a trip on your own, or want to supplement the information your travel agent has given you, there are many sources to check.

▲ Newspapers: Most larger papers have a special weekly section on travel. One of the best and most thorough is found in the Sunday edition of *The New York Times,* available at most libraries and some bookstores.
▲ Magazines: Three magazines that have consistently good and interesting travel articles are *Vogue, Gourmet,* and *Travel & Leisure.*
▲ Guidebooks: Although the number of guidebooks on the market increases dramatically every year, you'll find there are some good standbys, which are frequently the most idiosyncratic and interesting as well. A few that I've found useful for travel in the United States are:
   Let's Go U.S.A. by the Harvard Student Agencies, Inc. (St. Martin's Press). A basic budget guide.
   United States by Stephen Birnbaum (Houghton Mifflin). Updated every year and written in a vivid

style, it describes some out-of-the-way places and
sites.

Mobil Travel Guide (Rand McNally). Different editions
for various sections of the country; an indispensible
guide for a car trip, as it lists almost every motel and
restaurant along the way. Just don't take the rating
system too seriously.

Country Inns and Back Roads (The Berkshire Traveller
Press). Descriptions of old, charming, or rustic inns
and resorts for special vacations or stopovers.

For travel abroad, look for:

Michelin Green Guides (Michelin). Always reliable,
Michelin also publishes red guides to about twenty
cities, all small enough to fit in a pocket or handbag.

Frommer's Dollarwise Guides (Frommer/Pasman-
tier). A blessing for the budget-conscious.

Fodor's Travel Guides (McKay). Thorough and trustworthy.

Insight Guides (Apa Productions; distributed by
Prentice-Hall). A must if you're going to Asia.

Lonely Planet "Travel Survival Kits" (published in
Australia—by Lonely Planet Publications, PO Box
88, South Yarra, Victoria 3141, Australia—but
widely distributed here). Books for more out-of-
the-way places, for which a guidebook is essential,
like Burma, Sri Lanka, Pakistan, New Guinea. Especially useful for the shoestring traveler.

Tip: If you're an avid walker, then you'll want to
know about *WalkWays* (incorporating *Walking! Jour-*

nal). It's full of articles on health, walking tours throughout the world, books, and items of interest to people who love to walk. There's also a gift catalog of maps, bags, sticks, and other goodies in each issue. It costs ten dollars for one year (four issues) from WalkWays, 733 15th St. NW, Suite 427, Washington, DC 20005 (202-737-9555).

▲ If you have trouble finding good guidebooks, you can visit, call, or write to The Complete Traveller, 199 Madison Avenue, New York, NY 10016 (212-685-9007).

Personal planning. No matter who makes your basic travel arrangements, remember that it's *your* trip. Sit down with a piece of paper and mark it out in calendar spaces, one for each day of your trip. Fill in any activities you must, or want to, do. Make sure there are no conflicts, and make sure you leave plenty of time for actual travel (it's a good idea to avoid making appointments for the day of arrival) and for rest. There's nothing more anxiety-making than a jammed schedule, especially on a vacation.

Organize your travel information—brochures, maps, and books—by copying out pertinent information in a small notebook or memo pad. There's no need to take a few pounds of paper with you. You can also photocopy just those pages from a guidebook that describe places you want to visit, and leave the rest at home. You may not even need a whole map when a corner will do; carefully tear off the part you need.

This notebook is also the place to record things like phone numbers you'll need while you're gone (you don't need your whole address book), your insurance policy numbers, medical information, list of credit cards and numbers, and traveler's check numbers. Paste or tape an envelope in the back of the notebook for the bits and scraps you'll be bound to collect: addresses, cards, receipts, suggestions, and notes. Keep a few postcard and letter stamps here as well. You can save even more time and energy later by pre-addressing self-stick labels to friends and family now. Finally, this envelope is the place to keep extra passport-sized photos you may need when going abroad (more on this later).

Tip: If you don't have one already think now about getting a telephone credit card. You'll be able to make calls from phone booths without needing a pile of change or calling collect, and you can save a bundle by avoiding the hotel surcharge on calls made from your room.

Before you leave home. You should be aware of all the things that would shout to a potential burglar that you're away: milk and paper deliveries piling up, an overflowing mailbox. It's best to arrange for these details well before you leave:

▲ Cancel regular deliveries and have the post office or a neighbor hold your mail.
▲ Leave a house key and your itinerary with a neighbor.

▲ If you have your lawn mowed regularly, have it done while you're away as well.

▲ It's a good idea to put timers on some lights, and perhaps on a radio.

▲ If you're going to be gone a long time, you can have your phone service turned off (but be aware that the phone company can charge to have it turned back on); if you're not, turn down the bell as low as possible. In some cases, a thief who has you particularly in mind as a mark will phone your number from a nearby pay phone, leave it ringing, and go to your house to hear if the phone's been answered. If it hasn't, he knows you're gone. Answering machines may help to foil such enterprising burglars, but be sure your message doesn't reveal that no one's home, or that you're on vacation.

Now that you've set the scene, it's time to start getting your act together. And the key to that is your wardrobe.

GETTING YOUR ACT TOGETHER

If you've ever had to leave on a trip suddenly, chances are you found yourself with some missing links, and some mistakes, when you arrived. Maybe it was as simple as having forgotten your mascara (and you never like to go out without it), or merely as annoying as having to buy pantyhose at the hotel drugstore (an inferior brand at twice the price you normally pay). Or it could have been a disaster: Nothing you brought seemed to go with any-thing else, or the clothes you brought were all wrong for the occasion.

Some women pack for every trip on the spur of the moment, tossing clothes into the suitcase from the dresser drawers—"I guess I should bring three T-shirts, and I like this skirt"—and rifling through the medicine chest in a hurry. These women seldom look quite put together when they arrive. Sound familiar?

Since traveling light is about both knowing how to pack the *right,* as well as the fewest, pieces of clothing, and feeling certain about yourself every step of the way, it only stands to reason that it's a state that takes some forethought to achieve.

The preparation begins at home, as soon as possible— right now if you like. In fact, it's *better* to do it now than later. You can't wait until the day before the trip to organize everything and still expect it to come off right.

Remember the adage "a stitch in time saves nine"? Well, applying that—sometimes even literally—to your wardrobe, your cosmetics, and even your luggage right now will save you time and money later on.

After reading the wardrobe sections here, you'll have a pretty good idea about what you should look for. By starting early, you'll have time enough to comparison-shop for those items you need—and to find things you really *like.* And you can buy at sales and from mail-order catalogs with time to spare. The point is that you won't have to *settle* for anything; you'll be in control. And that's what our aim is here!

Tip: What's the key to building a versatile and ultimately inexpensive travel (or any other, for that matter) wardrobe? Keeping an eye out for—and buying—*double-duty* clothes. It's possible to find pieces that can take you smoothly from day to night, as well as from spring through fall. Fabric is pivotal: Light wool jersey is probably the most versatile choice. For example, a black jersey skirt or dress (in a simple style) is readily appropriate for day, and will be perfectly elegant for evening wear, too. So, as you forage through your closet and dresser drawers—and later, when you're shopping to fill in those gaps—keep the principle of double-duty dressing firmly in mind.

The closet situation. The first step in organizing your travel wardrobe is finding out what forgotten treasures lurk in the dark recesses of your closet and dresser drawers, and bringing them out into the light of day. If you vaguely recall a summer shift back there that you might want to recycle for beach weekends, you should find it *now.* Being able to pack quickly and painlessly depends not only on knowing what you own, but also on being sure that every single piece is ready to wear.

When in doubt, *try it on.* Now's the time to discover that you need a strapless bra with that slinky camisole, or that your favorite summer skirt seems to have grown an ink stain or two.

Have a sack ready for items that don't fit any more, are too out of fashion to be retailored, or are stained or worn beyond repair. These are candidates for the Salvation Army.

Next, pull out the clothes you've been meaning to repair—all those skirts with drooping hemlines, those blouses that are missing buttons, or those slacks with raveled seams—and *keep them out* until you sew them or have them sewn back to perfect condition. Anything that's destined for the dry cleaner should be taken at once.

Finally, you might want to rearrange your closet or your drawers according to season, if you have the space. With fewer items in your closet—only the ones you'll wear—you'll be able to see all your options at a glance, and you won't have to waste time right before a trip playing a guessing game.

The lingerie drawer. For many women, this is the black hole into which disappears the accumulation of years. Look at your pantyhose now, to make sure there are none with snags or runs. If you eliminate all the wounded pantyhose, you'll be able to pack practically in the dark. Ditto underwear. As for slips, toss the dingy ones that drag a quarter of an inch beneath your skirts—you'll never wear them anyway (you don't now, do you?). And take a few moments to go through your socks and get rid of any mateless ones; you'll never replace the missing one, and lone socks only take up room you need for other items.

The right foot. Especially when you travel for business, every detail counts, and this goes for shoes too. Take good care of your shoes and not only will they look better, they'll last longer. This means you must always keep shoes polished and heels in good repair. As one businesswoman puts it, "The top people in business *look* like the top people." Besides, what could be more annoying than having to run around a new town searching for the shoe repair? You've got better things to do with your travel time!

Accessories. Now that you've gotten adept at weeding and renovating your wardrobe, lingerie, and shoes, you should turn your attention to those invaluable little items that can make or break your outfit. The key here is to get rid of anything that no longer fits, is in bad repair, is terribly outdated, and/or doesn't go with anything you own.

▲ Belts: Fortunately, belts of all widths and styles have recently made a big fashion comeback. But do eliminate any of your old belts which have become worn, have tacky buckles, are too small or narrow. At the same time, consider the usefulness of sashes—scarves, cloth belts—and think of the possibility of making some by finishing the ends of interesting rectangles of fabric.

▲ Scarves: You can't have too many of these handy lifesavers—in all fabrics, colors, and sizes. You'll need scarves, and belts as well, to transform a minimal, light-traveling wardrobe into a wide variety of looks.

▲ Handbags: Most women hoard handbags, but be honest with yourself: If a bag is too big, too small, too bedraggled, too boxy, or too peculiar a color to be terribly versatile, give it away *now*. You have better use for the space!

▲ Jewelry: The ways of sorting out and organizing jewelry are as individual as the women who wear it. The point here is simply to know what you have and to eliminate useless and broken pieces. (But you know by now that fashion has a way of circling back: Try to save items that are still in good condition. Like this year's reappearance of large *faux* jewels, there may be another jewelry trend just around the corner that you could be well supplied for.)

It's inevitable that once you've been as ruthless as you ought, you'll see some gaps in your collection of usable accessories. Before you run out and buy more, reflect a moment on *why* you had to throw out so much in the first place: Were they bad purchases to begin with? If you tossed out items that were worn out because they were made of poor materials, fad buys that only got a wearing or two before they looked passé, or things you liked in the store but never used because they never seemed to go with anything you owned, then you must determine not to make the same mistake when you shop this time.

The key to the endeavor—for accessories and clothing

alike—is simple quality. That doesn't mean expensive, either: One good belt that you wear is cheaper by a lot than two that don't get worn. Here's a rundown of the most basic gap-fillers you should look for:

▲ a perfect blouse, in white or ivory
▲ two skirts for winter and two for summer, in the simplest cut your body can wear
▲ a cardigan sweater
▲ the best pump you can buy—with a mid-height heel, in summer and winter neutrals like brown, black, deep tan
▲ three scarves: a shawl-sized square, a basic square, and a rectangular sash
▲ a black or brown leather belt—a covered buckle eliminates jewelry-clashing problems
▲ a leather handbag or shoulder bag in black, brown, or tan
▲ jewelry that you love, in all types to compliment your looks

In chapter 2 we will discuss the finer points of a complete travel wardrobe. At this point, we simply want to discard anything and everything that has outlived its purpose, and to think about beginning to build a perfect, multifaceted wardrobe.

Your personal appearance needs the same kind of thought and preparation as your wardrobe to ensure hassle-free traveling. And you can apply the same techniques to evaluate and streamline your makeup and hair needs as you used with your wardrobe and accessories. Here are some ideas:

Hair. If you've been thinking about getting your hair cut, there's really no better time than now. Unkempt or too-long hair will definitely not contribute to a feeling of self-confidence. Think about trying one of the new, versatile "wash-and-wear" styles. Whether you travel for business or for pleasure, you don't want to waste time in the hotel room with curlers and hair spray (not to mention the waste of space in your luggage). There is now a great variety of hairstyles that take minimal time and effort to maintain. It's a good idea to go to a good—and trusted—hairdresser for a consultation before you decide to have it cut: Ask about a low-maintenance 'do that's right for your particular looks.

Another time- and space-waster involves having to shave legs and underarms, especially if you're taking a trip to the beach. Consider having legs and/or underarms waxed before you go—it costs about $35–50 for the works, and lasts up to six weeks. You can leave the razor and creams at home, and you won't have to think about shaving for the whole vacation.

Makeup. If you're like most people, your medicine chest is probably crammed with years of makeup trial and error. But that doesn't mean you have to bring that excess on a trip—or that it's OK because it's in such *little* tubes and jars. Traveling light, as I've said before, is traveling organized; you won't want to spend any more than the absolute minimum of time putting together great looks. And you don't have to.

Makeup can be just as important an accessory as a pearl necklace. But it's nice to know that drama can be created simply. There's no room for experimentation on a trip: Leave that for home. Basically, all you need is a day makeup and a night makeup. (On a sporting trip, of course, you need first and foremost makeup that protects your skin and lips from sun and wind.)

One top executive who travels a good deal always brings makeup in two color schemes: one (a warm tone) for, say, a beige suit, and another (a cooler tone) for a gray suit. Her makeup will adapt to any color accents she chooses to wear. By adding eyeliner and putting on slightly more makeup at night, all her needs are covered. And she uses makeup from the same line, shopping for it during special-offer sales when she can get travel-sized freebies as well.

At the moment, cosmetics companies are coming out with new items that can be a real boon to the traveler: lipstick and gloss in one; self-sharpening color pencils; complete color-coded makeup in one case. If you haven't shopped for anything new in a while, go and check out your options soon.

As with your wardrobe, if you weed out the outdated products from your bathroom chest, you'll be able to see clearly what you have, what you need, and what you should pack—at a glance.

Tip: Some frequent travelers keep a duplicate set of makeup and personal-care items in a toilet kit that's always ready to go. They replenish it upon return, and never have to think about it again until the next jaunt.

Now that we've gotten you organized—where you're going and who's handling the plans; clothing, accessories, and cosmetics all in order and ready to go—it's time to move on to the *real* challenge: choosing the right—and light—wardrobe for your trip.

2 Wardrobes to Go

EXTENDING THE BASICS—WEIGHTLESSLY

*H*ow many times have you overpacked? Well, don't feel bad; the complaint I hear most frequently from both business travelers and vacationers is that they just can't seem to get it right. Every trip, they vow to bring fewer articles of clothing but inevitably end up lugging around a whole slew of "extras" that never get worn—and despite the overload, they often complain that they didn't have anything to wear! You probably know from past experience that it's all too easy to go that route. That's why the *Traveling Light* wardrobe plans always center on versatility: Each piece can be worn at *least* two different ways, and usually more. The trick is to let

33

accessories—the lightweights—
forming basic clothing: It's easy
without adding significantly to the bulk you have to carry.

Color and style in a nutshell.

1. Solid colors are always more flexible than patterns, and they mix better. (It's difficult, too, to wear the same bright print shirt twice in a week without its being noticed.) Let your accessories add intricacy and detail to an outfit.

2. You don't need a different color of the rainbow for every occasion. When traveling, it's smartest to choose two, or three at the most, foundation colors that can be mixed, matched, and mated across the board—and stick to them. (You can always add new colors with your accessories.)

    While at first this may sound limiting, it is actually just the opposite. It means that *any* piece in your wardrobe can be "tossed together" with any other piece. Then add an accessory—a belt, scarf, or jewelry—for a new look. If you've chosen your basic pieces carefully, you'll find an infinite variety of possibilities.

    Here are some tried-and-true foundation combinations you can try:

While this type of color plan will work in many other combinations, the closer you stick to neutrals, the easier it will be to find the versatile pieces you need for travel when you shop.

CLOTHES	ACCESSORIES
black and white	red and turquoise
khaki and eggshell	earth tones
beige and tan	gold and ivory
grays and pinks	muted pastels

Once you're adept at the two-tone plan, you will find it extremely easy to introduce a third foundation color. Try adding bright turquoise to the black-and-white scheme, or rust to the khaki-and-eggshell combo. Basically, the more items that can be worn together, the fewer items you will have to bring with you.

I personally like black and white for my foundation colors. Black is a great travel color since it can be easily dressed up or down with accessories and doesn't show dirt. Almost any color will accent black and white dramatically. And black and white will always be chic, and always appropriate.

3. When you've confirmed your destination, check with guidebooks, friends, and/or travel agents about the clothing customs there. In the Greek islands, for instance, old women dress entirely in black, so you might not feel elegant or comfortable if you choose black as your foundation color. Similarly, you don't want to bring only sleeveless dresses and shorts to a

barred from religious or historical sites, and you might offend local residents.

4. *Simple clothes are more versatile.* It's hard (almost impossible!) to make a frilly evening dress work for daytime wear, but it's a snap to make a simply cut day dress work in the evening. Just as I said that simplicity in *color* choice is the foundation of a versatile wardrobe, the same is true of *style*. The more detailed a piece of clothing, the more difficult it is to add accessories: For instance, you may not be able to wear a belt with a dress that has strategically placed pockets or buttons. *Select simply styled garments.*

5. Don't skimp on the accessories—they're the hinges on which your wardrobe turns. Belts, scarves, jewelry, and hosiery are sure to transform a basic piece of clothing. Don't be afraid to experiment!

6. Monochromatic dressing needn't be boring—it can be dramatic! It more than doubles your options, if you follow the foundation-color system. Another plus: It can make you look taller and slimmer.

7. Fortunately, the best business look is the one that travels best: Simple separates in self-assured colors with a minimum of fussy tailoring make *you* look self-assured.

The illustrations here are only half the story. I guarantee that once you get the knack, you'll be able to create your own ways to vary the basic travel wardrobe. Just let your imagination go!

Fabric. Besides color and style, you should consider fabric when putting together your basic travel wardrobe. You want to be sure that your clothes will travel well with minimal care. For this reason, it's obvious that anything marked "Dry Clean Only" is not a good candidate for long-term travel: You won't be able to give it the simple once-over in the bathroom sink that traveling light often requires.

In natural fibers, your best bet is almost any kind of jersey material such as cotton or wool. These fabrics can be hand-washed in cold water, and they often don't need ironing at all—so long as you've blocked them out flat as they dry. And they can be rolled for easy packing (see chapter 4) in a soft bag.

In this day and age—and especially with travel in mind—it would be foolish to overlook the vast array of synthetics, because they were designed for easy maintenance. The main objection to most man-made fibers is that they don't "breathe" as well as natural ones. Depending on your travel plans, you might find this a small compromise to make for the gain in ease of care. A good synthetic silk look-alike can be washed out in the sink one night and be ready to wear the next morning without even getting close to an iron. Real silk, on the other hand, must usually be dry cleaned, or at best ironed *carefully* after hand-washing.

Many of the synthetic/natural blends are hard to distinguish from their natural counterparts. A pair of 50% polyester/50% cotton slacks or shorts, for instance, can look and feel as much like cotton as the real thing—and have the advantage of being completely wash-and-wear.

Whether or not you opt for synthetic garments is a matter of taste. But there is no doubt that man-made fibers are often ideal for the travel wardrobe.

The following chart will fill you in on the rest of the fabric story.

FABRIC	QUALITIES/CARE
cotton knit wool jersey	lightweight, wrinkle-proof, easy care; can be hand-washed and hung or blocked dry
wool gabardine	resists wrinkling fairly well, but may require dry cleaning
cotton	lightweight and cool; may need ironing
cotton velour	versatile for day and night; packs well; can be hand-washed and blocked dry
silk	lightweight; look for pieces that can be hand-washed; often needs ironing
raw silk	travels well, but usually requires dry cleaning

FABRIC	QUALITIES/CARE
cotton gauze	travels well, but is too casual to be versatile except on beach vacations; completely wash-and-wear
pure linen	classy fabric, but a travel problem: often needs dry cleaning and if not, always ironing; wrinkles easily
linen/viscose blend linen/Dacron or Fortrel	approximates the look of linen but travels better; can be hand- or machine-washed; needs ironing touch-ups
cotton/polyester blend	travels better than pure cotton but may not "breathe" as well in hot weather; usually wash-and-wear
rayon	a good traveler; breathes well; usually hand-washable; needs ironing touch-ups

THE WARDROBES

The Basic Wardrobe is designed to be the most fundamental travel wardrobe you can carry. These pieces are ideal for wear in almost any city, whether you are sightseeing or going to business appointments. We'll talk about how to transform these pieces for almost any occasion, and what to add to the wardrobe for longer trips, or for trips to different climates. This wardrobe can be modified to suit any woman, and will allow you to give free play to your own sense of style and creativity.

BASIC TRAVEL WARDROBE

The ideal fabric for most of these pieces is wool jersey, with tailored items in a light wool gabardine, for fall, winter, and early spring. Cotton knit is perfect for late spring, summer, and early fall. The pieces can be rolled and packed into a single soft-sided bag.

For a 3-to-5-day trip:

▲ one skirt (in a relatively straight or A-line cut)
▲ one straight-cut, simple dress
▲ one loose-fitting collarless (or similarly simple) blouse or shirt
▲ one pair of slacks
▲ one simple jacket
▲ reefer-style overcoat for winter wear; basic trench-style raincoat (with zip-out lining) for other seasons and climates

Remember to keep your foundation colors in mind when selecting these basic items.

For other daytime looks, try slipping the shirt under the dress, or the skirt over the dress (depending on the cut and fabric of each—lightweight, straight-cut clothes work best in this case); give the dress a blouson look by cinching the waist with a belt and blousing the dress over it slightly.

For a 7-to-9-day trip, add to the basic wardrobe:

▲ a deep-V cardigan sweater (in cashmere or thinly knit wool for cold weather, in cotton or cotton/silk knit for warm weather)
▲ a band-neck or other simple-collared silk or silk-like blouse in a neutral tone like ivory

The sweater can be worn as another jacket over the blouse with skirt or pants, and at night it can be worn backwards (the deep V shows off a sexy bit of back!) over the skirt.

For a 10-to-15-day trip, add:

▲ a simple round- or V-necked sweater (in cotton or wool)
▲ one more blouse
▲ one more skirt (of a different style and length from the first)

Warm-weather changes. If the climate of your destination is particularly hot or humid, you can bring the

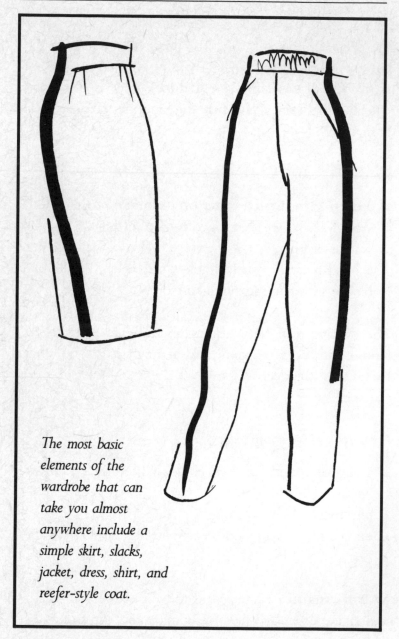

The most basic
elements of the
wardrobe that can
take you almost
anywhere include a
simple skirt, slacks,
jacket, dress, shirt, and
reefer-style coat.

THE TRANSFORMATIONS

DAYTIME

If the colors, fabrics, and cuts are right together, try the dress over the skirt for a long, lean look.

DAYTIME

The perfect look for daytime sightseeing or for business appointments is often the most simple, like the dress with an interesting belt, worn with lightly tinted hose.

DAYTIME

For another daytime look, pair the shirt with the skirt, add dash with earrings.

DAYTIME

For comfort and ease, you can't beat the casual chic of the jacket with a shirt and slacks.

NIGHTTIME

The simplest—and most luxe—look for night is to add dash to the basic dress with a stunning shawl and pearls.

THE TRANSFORMATIONS

DAYTIME

For a longer trip, bring a cardigan and another blouse to team with slacks for an easy daytime outfit.

NIGHTTIME

The same cardigan worn backwards with the skirt can take you out at night with style.

dress in a sleeveless version, and exchange the silky blouse for a second jersey T-shirt with three-quarter-length sleeves and a scoop or V-neck. Leave the reefer coat at home, of course, but don't forget the cardigan sweater— just bring it in a light cotton material.

For basic accessories the minimal list should include:

▲ a leather belt for day (or a straw or cloth belt for tropical climates)
▲ two silky scarves
▲ pearls or other dressy beads
▲ earrings for daytime wear and nighttime drama
▲ textured and colored pantyhose for day, tinted sheer hose for night

Basic shoe needs should be covered by two pairs:

▲ 1½- to 2-inch heeled pumps (or Chanel-type slingbacks) in black
▲ flat or nearly flat leather walking shoes

In summer, those flats could be sandals, and if you're going to be going out to dressy spots at night, you'll want to bring a pair of evening sandals as well. (See page 80, "All About Accessories," for more details.)

"HARD-CORE" BUSINESS WARDROBE

For some business trips, the basic wardrobe shown here is too casual. Certain businesswomen, especially those in finance, must stick to a narrower dress code, in which suits are the order of the day. If you are such a businesswoman, don't overlook my seven fashion points at the beginning of this chapter; just adapt them to your professional dress code. Suits should be simply tailored and in basic colors, like gray, beige, or navy. Blouses should be kept simple too, although silk or a silk look-alike is the best bet for the material. If at least two of these blouses have small or no collars, you can also bow-tie a rectangular scarf about the neck for a feminine touch. Don't forget that monochromatic dressing for business can be elegant as well as a statement of confidence. Your business clothes should be carried *only* in a folding garment bag.

For a 3-day business trip:

▲ one suit
▲ two blouses
▲ one dress or dress suit

For a 5-to-7-day business trip:

▲ two suits
▲ three or four blouses
▲ one dress

Additions. If your profession applies the business suit dress code, your daytime choices will be fairly limited. The real challenge here is dressing up the conservative wardrobe for evening wear. If you're going out at night as well, bring a simple straight or A-line dress (but nothing revealing, especially if you'll be seeing your business colleagues) as well as a cashmere or fine wool cardigan sweater.

Accessories.

▲ classic and understated jewelry—pearls; bar, circle, or stylishly simple pin; simple gold or pearl earrings
▲ at least two rectangular scarves (just long enough to tie a bow around the neck)
▲ two pairs of pumps, and perhaps higher heels for night
▲ stockings for day wear (must generally be neutral); black sheer hose for evening wear with black skirt or dress

"LIGHTWEIGHT" BUSINESS WARDROBE

Many professions don't require suits—just well put-together and businesslike outfits. That's easy to do if you select clothes carefully.

For a 5-day trip:

▲ one simple dress (in a tone like beige, gray, or black)
▲ one loose-constructed jacket

(cont. on p. 56)

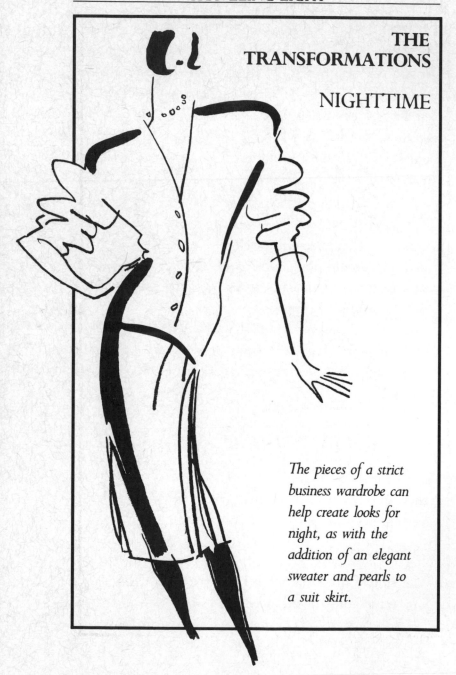

THE TRANSFORMATIONS

NIGHTTIME

The pieces of a strict business wardrobe can help create looks for night, as with the addition of an elegant sweater and pearls to a suit skirt.

NIGHTTIME

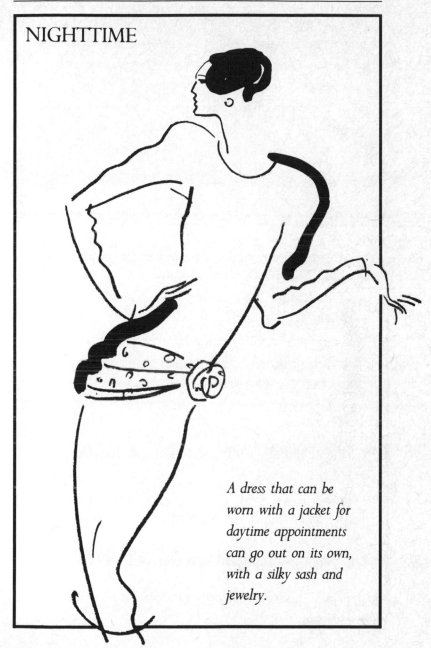

A dress that can be worn with a jacket for daytime appointments can go out on its own, with a silky sash and jewelry.

▲ one straight-cut or similarly tailored-looking skirt

▲ one longer, slightly fuller skirt—this one could be in an understated print, like a muted stripe, herringbone, or tweed

▲ two blouses or shirts (one of which should be white or off-white)

▲ one cardigan sweater

Other options.

▲ wear each skirt with either the cardigan or the jacket alone

▲ try the cardigan backwards under the jacket (for the look of a pullover)

▲ wear each skirt alone with a blouse and belt (no jacket or cardigan)

▲ wear the dress alone with a belt (no jacket or cardigan)

▲ wear the dress with either jacket or cardigan

▲ drape the shawl elegantly over the dress

Accessories.

▲ two leather belts (different widths and styles)

▲ two silky scarves

▲ one shawl

▲ pearls or beads; simple earrings

▲ textured and sheer hose

▲ one pair of pumps and one pair of flats

Best of all, this whole wardrobe can be packed in soft-sided luggage.

THE TRANSFORMATIONS

DAYTIME

An easygoing business look is achieved with a shirt, jacket, belt, and skirt.

DAYTIME

A cardigan over a simple dress can be an easy, but authoritative, look for meetings.

NIGHTTIME

The same dress shows
its basic drama at
night with the simple
addition of a luxurious
scarf and important-
looking jewelry.

WORK/PLAY COMBINATION WARDROBE

Often, our trips aren't clearly demarcated as strictly business or pleasure. There are going to be times when you have to move faster than you already do, and go directly from a week of business appointments to a weekend of fun—or mix an evening of casual frolic with a day of business. With a few additions to a basic wardrobe, you can actually make it easy.

For a 7-day combination trip, start with either the Basic Wardrobe or the "Lightweight" Business Wardrobe and add:

▲ knee-length walking shorts that can be rolled up or down (for warm weather) and/or a pair of jeans or khakis
▲ one or two T-shirts (one extra-large to wear as a bathing suit cover-up and/or nightshirt)
▲ a casual skirt
▲ a bandanna
▲ a pair of sneakers
▲ bathing suit

THE WEEKEND GETAWAY

What should you pack for a weekend away when you have to leave directly from the office? It's simple, really—

and it all fits into a small shoulder bag. The clothes described here will work for any warm-weather weekend.

For a 3-day trip:

▲ one skirt
▲ one pair of slacks
▲ one pair of shorts
▲ one blouse
▲ one jacket
▲ one sweater
▲ bathing suit
▲ two T-shirts (one extra-large to wear as bathing suit cover-up and/or nightshirt)
▲ sneakers
▲ a pair of pumps or flats

On the day you leave, wear the skirt, blouse, jacket, a neutral belt, and pumps (or flats) to work and stash the rest. If you'll be needing an evening outfit, pack a T-shirt shift and sandals.

Cold weather changes:

▲ a pair of jeans instead of shorts
▲ a cotton pullover or another sweater
▲ cotton turtleneck instead of a T-shirt
▲ boots or warm shoes instead of sneakers

BEACH/RESORT WARDROBE

A week-long trip to a beach resort in the Caribbean, Mexico, or Southern US makes two demands on a traveler: cool, comfortable, fun clothes for day, and a bit of drama at night. The clothes described here are bound to do the trick. Here's the perfect opportunity to be inventive with accessories—go all out if you like!

For a 7-day trip:

▲ two bathing suits
▲ one pareo (a piece of material approximately 1½ by 2 yards, with multiple uses, some of which are illustrated here)
▲ cotton skirt (may have elastic waistband)
▲ one sleeveless shift
▲ one pair of shorts
▲ four T-shirts of varying styles
▲ one sweater
▲ one shawl
▲ one windbreaker or similar jacket (for nighttime beach walks)
▲ one pair of cotton slacks

You can add blue jeans if you're the sporting type (or if you just like to walk on the beach a lot), and sneakers. If you need a beach cover-up, bring another sleeveless shift or an extra-large T-shirt or oversized man's shirt, any of which can also double as a nightie.

Tip: If you're going bathing suit-shopping before you go, keep in mind that Lycra is the fastest-drying material. And don't forget to rinse the salt or chlorine out of your suit each night—it'll make the fabric last longer.

Accessories.

▲ colorful jewelry (beads, wooden bangles, dramatic earrings)
▲ at least two large cotton scarves, brightly colored
▲ colorful sash for your waist
▲ flat and heeled sandals
▲ rubber thongs (great for poolside and/or instead of slippers)

Don't forget your sunglasses! And in tropical weather you'd be smart to include a hat (preferably with visor) to protect yourself from too much sun. You'll also need a bag to tote your things to the beach—the most lightweight idea is a French string marketing sack.

EUROPEAN TOUR WARDROBE

One of the most difficult trips to pack for is a sightseeing trip to major European cities. The biggest problem is how to be comfortable and look stylish at the same time. You

THE TRANSFORMATIONS

DAYTIME

*Don't overlook the
possibility of creating a
new, fun outfit with
two of the T-shirts
you've brought, in
different styles, worn
one over the other.*

DAYTIME

From beach to bar is more than easy with a quick wrap of the pareo.

DAYTIME

The same T-shirt you saw before goes under a shift for a spirited warm-weather look.

NIGHTTIME

*Nighttime in resort
towns calls for impact,
and a bare T-shirt
with skirt and sash
does the trick.*

NIGHTTIME

Your daytime dress will make waves at night on its own if it's spiced with bold accessories.

HOW TO WRAP A PAREO

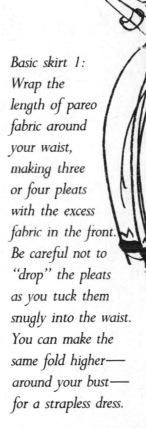

Pareos are indispensable for warm-weather vacations. They pack like a dream, make great bathing suit cover-ups, and can be worn in numerous ways. Aside from their fashion potential, they can always double as lightweight beach or picnic blankets and can be tied into makeshift knapsacks. Illustrated here are a few of my favorite pareo fashion wraps. Once you get the hang of it, it's easy to come up with more. The only limitation is your imagination.

Basic skirt 1: Wrap the length of pareo fabric around your waist, making three or four pleats with the excess fabric in the front. Be careful not to "drop" the pleats as you tuck them snugly into the waist. You can make the same fold higher— around your bust— for a strapless dress.

HOW TO WRAP A PAREO

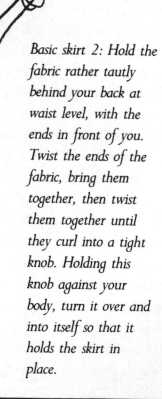

Basic skirt 2: Hold the fabric rather tautly behind your back at waist level, with the ends in front of you. Twist the ends of the fabric, bring them together, then twist them together until they curl into a tight knob. Holding this knob against your body, turn it over and into itself so that it holds the skirt in place.

HOW TO WRAP A PAREO

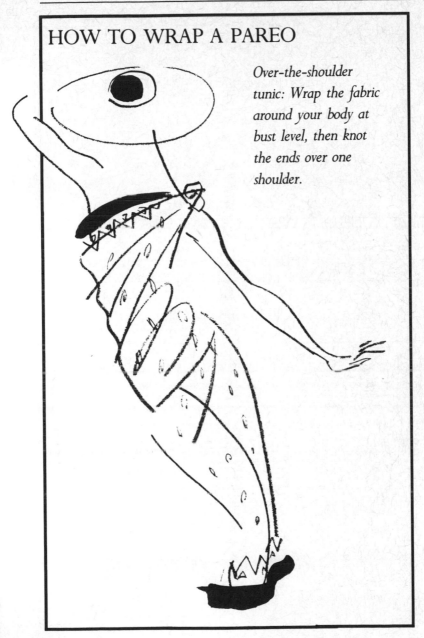

Over-the-shoulder tunic: Wrap the fabric around your body at bust level, then knot the ends over one shoulder.

HOW TO WRAP A PAREO

Crisscross tunic: Wrap the pareo high up around your back, so you can hold the ends out in front of you. Then cross the ends in front of you and bring them around to tie behind your neck.

HOW TO WRAP A PAREO

Butterfly shawl: Fold the pareo in two lengthwise. Tie the corners together into small knots at each end to create a sort of tube. With the folded edge on top, drape the material over your shoulders, then put your arms through the open edge at the bottom, and out again to the side. You can use a pareo to make a simple shawl as well, by folding the fabric into a triangle.

frequently leave your hotel in the morning, walk all day, and go out to dinner at night without being able to stop back at the hotel for a quick change of clothing, so you'll need to carry all your transforming accessories with you.

Most of all, you want to look like you *belong,* not look like a tourist. Blue jeans and running shoes are out— they'll label you "tourist" at a glance, and they're too difficult to transform. Follow these guidelines instead, and pay attention to the discussion of accessories that follows this wardrobe section.

For a 14-day trip:

▲ two pairs of slacks
▲ two dresses (one should be scoop- or V-necked if possible)
▲ two skirts
▲ one cardigan
▲ one loose-styled jacket
▲ two blouses
▲ two T-shirts

The best color scheme for these items is black and white, adding perhaps a couple of pieces in bright blue or red. To me, black and white are more sophisticated, more elegant, than many other basic color combinations. But if you prefer, navy, gray, or tan can also form a solid ground on which to build a functional wardrobe. It's especially important on a trip like this to keep colors basic—

simplicity is elegance, and the dark colors will hide dirt and mix together well.

For daytime, you'll need a sturdy shoulder bag that can carry a change of shoes, a scarf and some jewelry, a smaller evening bag, cosmetics, comb, brush, and collapsible umbrella (if the weather tends to be wet). If it's chilly, wear a raincoat (with or without lining); if not, tuck a shawl into your bag for the evening.

Accessories. The most important item(s) you will bring on a trip like this will be your shoes. You must have two pairs of *comfortable* walking shoes, and one pair of pumps for evening wear. Also bring

▲ a shawl
▲ pearls or beads, and a selection of simple earrings
▲ plenty of hosiery and socks (at least four pairs of each)
▲ four silky scarves—two square and two rectangular
▲ two belts

SKI WEEKEND

If you're a seasoned skier, you already know what to bring as far as specialized clothing. But if it's your first time out on the slopes, you should be aware that you will need to put out some money for a few items of ski clothes. You can't do without these basics:

THE TRANSFORMATIONS

DAYTIME TO NIGHTTIME

The daytime dress-with-blouse changes into the evening glamour of a dress and pearls. The trick: Remove blouse, change shoes, add pearls and makeup.

THE TRANSFORMATIONS

DAYTIME TO NIGHTTIME

You don't need to go back to the hotel to make this change; just take off the blouse over the shirt, and dress up the pants with a silky scarf for the evening.

▲ stretch ski pants
▲ leather or suede ski mittens or gloves
▲ goggles or special sunglasses

For a 3-day trip:

▲ two pairs of thick socks
▲ two pairs of thin socks
▲ two cotton turtlenecks
▲ one or two thick pullover sweaters
▲ one set of long underwear
▲ hat or earmuffs
▲ parka or ski shell

Depending on the kind of resort, for night you will also need either casual clothes—blue jeans or slacks and a pretty sweater or two—or something dressier—a flannel or wool dress or a skirt and sweater, pumps, and tights. Short, warm, waterproof boots are the best idea for maneuvering icy parking lots and runs to the hot chocolate stand.

A THREE-DAY HIKE

In backpacking, your primary concern can't be fashion: It must be comfort, warmth, and safety. Still, with all the great looks you'll find in your local army-navy store, you may be tempted to wear your hiking clothes on the street—so you're sure to look wonderful in the woods too.

If this is your first trip, you should begin your planning by consulting a specialized backpacking guidebook and by talking to more experienced members of your group and a knowledgeable salesperson at an outdoors store. Nowhere is traveling light more important than on a hike, when you must carry all your belongings with you at all times—and nowhere are you more restricted by what you must bring. These are the basics.

For a 3-day hike:

▲ *most important* are well-fitting, broken-in boots or hiking shoes with right-weight socks
▲ one pair of long pants (jeans or other sturdy type)
▲ two wool shirts or sweaters
▲ waterproof parka
▲ three pairs of socks
▲ hat or cap (one with a visor would be good)
▲ sweatpants and sweatshirt

Tip: If the weather is likely to be wet, you should bring wool clothing, which is the only fabric that will retain heat when wet.

Non-clothing essentials:

▲ sleeping bag (appropriate weight for the climate)
▲ lightweight camping blanket

- ▲ cookware and food
- ▲ Swiss Army knife
- ▲ firestarter (fire ribbon or fuel tablets)
- ▲ water- and wind-proof matches
- ▲ first aid kit and manual
- ▲ flashlight
- ▲ compass
- ▲ two bandannas

ALL ABOUT ACCESSORIES

By now, you've noticed the emphasis placed on accessories and their ability to transform basic outfits for almost any purpose. The following discussions of the ins and outs of working with the proper extras begin with what may turn out to be your most important "accessory" for comfort, well-being, and looks: your shoes.

Shoes. The first choice of many working women is a medium-heeled pump. That's because it's impossible to look professional while teetering on high-high heels—not to mention the fact that carrying bags or walking long distances wearing these shoes can be a painful experience. So you should stay away from them, except for evening wear, when higher heels are fine.

Since shoes are heavy, you can't bring a wardrobe of different colors with you. If you follow the general advice on color in the wardrobe descriptions, your first choice might be a pair of black pumps. (For the lighter color schemes, and in warm weather, tan would be a good choice.) Flat walking shoes look best in a basic brown.

If you are able to wear more unstructured clothes for work (as in the basic or "lightweight" wardrobes), you might want to select a brown brogan for cold-weather wear—they're back in fashion and are great for walking. If you feel you need to wear a slightly higher heel, there are versions of this shoe with 1½- to 2-inch heels.

For evening wear, unless the climate is snowy, medium- to high-heeled sandals can be worn in either summer or winter. For warm weather, look for a flat sandal with a touch of gold or bronze that can be worn for day, too. But your basic black pumps can do evening duty in almost any season: Buy some grosgrain ribbon clips (available at shoe stores) for either the front or the back of shoes—it's a bit of quick-change magic you can carry in the smallest purse.

For sporting vacations, you'll want to add some form of sneaker. If you play tennis, avoid leather shoes, which are heavy. Instead, choose a canvas shoe that can be used for walking and for other sports as well. If you want to run or jog, you do need to bring shoes specifically for that.

At the beach, rubber thongs from a five-and-dime can be indispensable (and light!) for going to and from the beach or pool, and for use as slippers. Speaking of slippers, in my opinion they're a waste of space, because they have only one function. Rubber thongs can do double duty as slippers if you're staying in a bed-and-breakfast, someone else's home, or an inexpensive pension—any place where the bathroom is down the hall.

Flat espadrilles can be worn at the beach and can double as slippers. But don't make the mistake of depending on them for major walking expeditions. You'll only end up with aching feet, because these shoes can't give the support or cushioning you need to walk on hard surfaces. The same drawback holds for Chinese slippers (the cotton ones with thin rubber soles), as well as for rubber "jellies"—although the latter are useful for quick rainy-day jaunts.

In some third-world countries, it's not a good idea to wear sandals at all, as any cut on your feet could land you with a major infection. Instead, wear sneakers or solid rubber flats when normal covered shoes won't do.

Finally, there's the problem of foul-weather shoes. Unless you're going to a snowy climate, leave boots at home. If you plan to encounter some slush or lots of rain, bring a fold-up pair of slip-on rubbers.

The very last word: *Never* bring brand-new shoes on a trip. Make sure they're well broken-in!

Handbags. For daytime, casual activities, sightseeing, and an easy-going business look, you need a sturdy and reasonably large bag, either leather or good-looking canvas with leather trim. It should be simple in design. Black or brown are the best color choices. If you also carry a briefcase, the daytime bag should be smaller.

For evening, choose a single fabric or leather clutch that can hold all your necessities, but which can also fit into your daytime bag for quick evening changes when you can't return to your hotel (check the large bag at the coat check).

Tip: Use your evening bag as a sack for your jewelry when you pack.

Scarves and shawls. These lightweight bits of fabric can turn out to be your best friends on a trip. The most useful scarves are silk or a silky synthetic, which are practically weightless. As you've seen, they can literally transform a look, if the basic clothes are simple enough.

Almost any scarf size is the right size, but here are some ideas:

▲ For day, loosely bow-tie a rectangular scarf (about a yard long) around the neck of a simple band-neck blouse for a finished look.

▲ At night, a long, silky scarf (about 8″ by 56″) around the waist of a simple, straight dress will transform the look; a particularly charming idea is to knot a scarf like a wide sash low on the hips, with a bow in the back. This same extra-long scarf can do double duty as an elegant neck-tie for another outfit.

▲ Two solid-color sashes can be twisted together to form a colorful rolled-band belt.

▲ Casual cotton squares (in sizes from 22″ to 26″—

much smaller than that and there's not much more to do with it than stick it in a pocket) are great for sporty trips: You can roll and tie one around your head when playing tennis or hiking; tie one around the waist of your bathing suit while you're sunning; knot a colorful one around the neck of a white T-shirt for a cool, sporty accent.

▲ For warmer climates, don't forget to bring a shawl (about 45″ square) to provide your evening glamour, as well as to stave off the chill that comes with sundown or in air-conditioned rooms. In winter, you can make a shawl a part of either day or night outfits by securing it with a circle or bar pin. Challis, warm yet lightweight, is a good year-round, packable material for shawls.

▲ As you've seen illustrated on pages 69–73, pareos can be lifesavers. With the simple addition of sandals and some jewelry, this piece of cloth can wrap around your bathing suit and take you to lunch or drinks. It can be used as a shawl at night, or it can even double as a bathrobe-like cover-up.

Tip: Before you leave, you might want to visit your local dimestore for a package of all-cotton, extra-large men's handkerchiefs. You can tie them around your head or your waist as a simple sash, and you'll have extras to use as hankies, as napkins for impromptu picnics, and in so many other ways.

Nightclothes. If you're used to sleeping in the nude, you're already on your way to being a light traveler! If not, though, do bring what you like to wear—trips aren't times to make yourself uncomfortable by trying something new. But you might consider replacing your nightie with an oversized T-shirt that can also double as a mini-shift or bathing suit cover-up as well.

Bathrobes are another story, however. Most of them are simply too bulky and infrequently worn to justify their weight. If you're staying at a friend's house or in a hotel room where the bathroom is down the hall, you might want a robe of some sort; look for a silk or light cotton kimono robe. By substituting a belt for the sash, a robe like this (in a dark, "unbedroom-y" color) can even work as a beach cover-up or sporty dress.

Hosiery. Don't forget that pantyhose can be a great (and *very* lightweight) fashion transformer. For daytime wear in cold climates, thick or textured stockings add both interest and warmth. You can find some wonderful cable-knit versions that will keep you really toasty, and they look especially good with flat walking shoes.

Before you leave, experiment with new colors: Burgundy and ivory hose will go well with the Basic Wardrobe here, and black can be elegant at night. It's better to err on the side of abundance when you're packing pantyhose, because it may be difficult to find the right size, color, and brand you like in a new town (and *very* difficult in Europe).

Jewelry. Another great thing about wearing simple clothing in solid colors is that it provides a wonderful backdrop for dramatic jewelry. And it doesn't have to be real or expensive to be effective: In fact, it's not a good idea to bring real jewelry on a trip in the first place. The good news is that there's been a revolution in what's known as costume jewelry recently, and designers like Anne Klein and Yves St. Laurent have created lines of reasonably priced *faux* jewels. For a more toned-down business look, Monet and Trifari have always made subdued, gold-toned pieces.

Your most versatile decoration could well turn out to be a strand of cultured or fake pearls. They have a perennially fresh look, and will instantly dress up almost any outfit.

The point is not to go overboard, though. If you choose one striking piece (say, a marvelous necklace) don't divert attention from it with large earrings *and* sparkly bracelets. Wear small earstuds instead. Likewise, if you have a pair of dramatic earrings, sweep your hair away from your face and let them shine, but don't wear a big necklace too. Wear some wonderful bracelets—or wrap a necklace around your wrist! Like scarves and hosiery, jewelry gives a lightweight, easy opportunity to change the tone of your appearance. Have fun with it.

Belts. You can rely on belts to re-create a look. A simple, straight dress like the one in the Basic Wardrobe can be cinched for day with a woven leather belt, or with one of the new thick leather belts worn low on the hips. The same dress at night with a silk sash or a draped shawl takes on a lighter, more elegant look.

For a week-long trip, bring at least two belts, in different widths and colors, that will work with dress, skirt, and slacks. Bring at least one evening sash or rectangular silk scarf—more if your evening schedule is heavy.

Lingerie. For a week-long or longer trip, you'll need at least two bras, four panties, and a half or full slip. Do make certain you've brought any special underwear (strapless or low-cut bras, for example) you need. When you pack as conservatively as this, don't forget to bring soap powder in small packets or in a plastic bag that you've filled yourself. If you don't like to wash underwear by hand, bring as many panties as days you'll be gone.

Hats. Unfortunately, many hats are simply a waste of precious space. But that doesn't mean you have to go bareheaded! For winter warmth, here are three great-looking, space-saving options: a French beret (packs flat!); a knit cloche worn low over the eyes; an extra-large wool or challis muffler—place over head, wrap under chin, around to back and tie—scarf and hat in one!

Tip: For beach trips or jaunts to tropical climes, don't forget to pack some sort of head covering (golf caps are fine and roll up easily): Too much sun can literally make you sick. Some resorts sell cheap straw hats; it might make sense to buy one and discard it when you leave, rather than waste valuable luggage room.

Coats and cover-ups. When traveling from a cold climate to a warm one, or vice versa, you must think of how the largest part of your time will be spent. It doesn't make sense to bring a heavy wool coat to Sea Island, no matter *how* cold it is in Iowa when you leave. A much better idea is a trench coat with a zip-out lining—you can use it on the trip if it rains. Or you can layer: a cardigan sweater over another sweater—either one alone will be useful on a midnight walk on the beach, and you'll leave home as warm as you would in a coat that would sit in your vacation closet unused.

A cardigan sweater can be one of the most versatile pieces in any travel wardrobe. For women who can wear more loosely structured clothes for business, a cardigan can give the polish of a jacket over a skirt or slacks. If it's cashmere, angora, or a blend, the same sweater can create a dazzling nighttime look with the addition of a simple silk blouse and pearls. For a more daring look, the right cardigan can be worn backwards, without a shirt, to bare the back with a deep V. A light pastel or ivory color would work best for day and night.

Even in summer, a cardigan or light jacket is essential to cope with evening breezes and air-conditioned buildings. For this season, it can be a lighter wool jersey, or a cotton knit (one mixed with silk is particularly soft).

If you're going to one of the places I've listed in the Temperature/Climate Guide as "frequently rainy," you should always bring a raincoat. If you're looking to buy a new one, the classic trench with zip-out lining is still the best, and most versatile, bet. Think about getting a black one; dirt doesn't show here as it does on a tan one. Leave the lining at home if you're traveling to warmer places.

A slicker or poncho is a boon for weekends at a country house, and a poncho is a must for camping trips (it should be large enough to fit over the pack on your back). For most other trips, however, these coats are too casual.

Finally, unless you're going to a spot which is known to be very dry, a collapsible umbrella is essential.

Temperature/Climate Guide

US CITY	AVERAGE WINTER LOWS/ SUMMER HIGHS (° F)	CONDITIONS
Atlanta	35/85	rainy winters; humid summers
Boston	20s/80s	harsh winters; humid summers
Chicago	20/80s	fierce winter wind chill; muggy summers
Cleveland	20/80s	cold, snowy winters; humid summers
Dallas	45/100	rainy winters; dry, hot summers
Denver	20s/85	fairly dry
Detroit	20/80	sudden weather changes

US CITY	AVERAGE WINTER LOWS/ SUMMER HIGHS (° F)	CONDITIONS
Honolulu	65/85	frequent brief showers
Houston	40s/90s	humid summers
Indianapolis	20s/80s	humid summers
Los Angeles	50s/80s	fairly dry; foggy and smoggy
Memphis	35/90s	wet winters; humid summers
Miami	60/85	lots of sun
Milwaukee	10/80	windy
Minneapolis	10/80	extremely cold winters
Nashville	35/85	frequently rainy
New Orleans	40/90	wet and humid
New York	28/80s	be prepared for rain; humid summers
Omaha	10/90s	frequent brief summer showers
Philadelphia	25/80s	humid summers
Phoenix	40/90s	usually dry
Pittsburgh	20s/80s	frequent precipitation, year-round
Portland	35/80	lots of rain
St. Louis	20s/80s	hot, humid, rainy summers
Salt Lake City	20/90	dry; snowy winters

San Antonio	50/90s	sunny; occa-sional thunderstorm
San Diego	50/70	fairly dry
San Francisco	45/75	changeable; foggy
Savannah	50/90s	fairly rainy
Seattle	30s/75	moderate; fairly wet
Washington, DC	30/80s	humid summers; often rainy

FOREIGN DESTINATION	AVERAGE WINTER LOWS/ SUMMER HIGHS (° F)	CONDITIONS
Amsterdam	37/64	frequently rainy
Athens	52/90	rainy winters; hot summers
Bali	82	hot; dry May through Sept.; rainy Oct. through April
Bangkok	62/98	tropical year round; rainy June to Oct.
Beijing	25/77	dry, cold winters; wet summers
Berlin	10/75	fairly wet
Buenos Aires	57/85	seasons reversed from US
Cairo	65/90	hot, dry summers

FOREIGN DESTINATION	AVERAGE WINTER LOWS/ SUMMER HIGHS (° F)	CONDITIONS
Copenhagen	32/66	frequently rainy
Dublin	40/61	frequently rainy
Frankfurt	32/70	temperate; cold in winter
Hong Kong	40/90	extremely humid summers
Kathmandu	30s/80s	hot summers; cool winters; rainy June to Oct.
Lisbon	46/90s	fairly dry
London	39/64	be always prepared for rain
Madrid	41/75	hot, dry summers
Moscow	13/80s	long, cold winters; moderate precipitation
New Delhi	50s/90s	cool Oct. through Feb.; hot, dry April, May; rainy June through Sept.
Nice	47/80s	fairly sunny year round
Paris	35/74	often rainy
Rio de Janeiro	60s/90s	seasons reversed from US
Rome	46/80s	mild, rainy winters; hot summers

Singapore	74/87	warm and sunny; rainy Nov. to Jan.
Sydney	50/73	seasons reversed from US
Tangier	50/80	mild winters; dry, sunny summers
Tokyo	38/77	frequently rainy
Vienna	30/67	snowy winters
Zurich	30/59	fairly wet

3 Luggage

GETTING THE BEST YOU CAN

n ow that you're ready to go, what are you going to pack your clothes in? At last, it seems, luggage companies have caught on to the fact that we appreciate a bit of choice—and a more up-to-date look. No longer does the green molded-vinyl suitcase, serviceable though it was, suit all our needs. Though we got the picture from the television commercials that our luggage wasn't exactly treated with t.l.c. by the airlines (remember the one that showed a gorilla throwing the bags around after they disappeared behind the ticket counter?), we have been allowed to discover that there are alternatives to steel-plated luggage for safety. Now the only problem we've got is too much choice! What should you look for in what's currently on the market? Before I give you some guidelines, I'll tell you my golden rule: If you buy cheap, that's just what you'll get.

Chances are that if you're interested in traveling light you'll also be interested in soft luggage. You'll be looking at a lot of canvas and nylon bags. But there are also degrees of softness: American Tourister, for instance, has developed new lines of soft-sided luggage that have thicker vinyl edges and bottoms (some with "bumper feet") and metal frames. Pieces like this retain their shape whether they're packed or not, but expand in a way that hard luggage can't. On the other end of the soft spectrum are completely collapsible pieces, some of which weigh only a few ounces and have no interior structure of their own. They're basically sacks with zippers. Your basic travel needs have to determine your choice.

A simple word of caution: *Never* buy a bag that isn't fully waterproof. I guarantee that you'll be sorry if you do. Even on a dry day in New Mexico, baggage handlers have the uncanny ability to find a puddle for your bags to sit in. And traveling anywhere in the winter is bound to do nasty things to a bag that isn't prepared. Finally, treated material resists the natural accumulation of dirt that can make the most carefully put-together traveler look a mess.

The table on pages 98–99, which mentions some well-known brand names (although most major companies make similar products in a broad range) is arranged from deluxe on down. Again, remember that expensive doesn't necessarily mean better, but truly cheap always means just that.

Your first step should be to go to a reputable dealer, one who sells brands whose names you recognize, who will stand behind his products and their warranties. Tell the dealer what you're looking for, and describe your range of needs—whether you travel frequently or not, for short hops or long hauls, for business or pleasure, by plane or ship or train, and so on. Don't forget to mention restrictions on your storage space, either. Don't settle for what the store has in stock at the moment. It's always a good idea to take your time and shop around.

As for looks, while aesthetics are certainly important, you don't need to buy expensive leather to look well put-together. Convenience and quality are the two factors that should guide you. In the end, unless you have a special desire for deluxe luggage, mid-priced luggage from a trustworthy manufacturer is the best investment for comfortable and safe travel. If you travel on business and want to splurge, you'd be better off putting your money into an exceptional briefcase.

No matter what type of luggage you choose, you need to know what signals good construction. Here are the elements you should check for:

▲ In any leather luggage, look for uniform thickness in the leather. Belting leather is especially strong. Make certain there's no cracking around the edges, where the leather has been bent around the frame; this indicates low-grade material. Good leather bags are very expensive. If you find a relatively inexpensive leather bag, you need to look carefully at every element of the construction to see where the cost has been trimmed.

▲ When looking at nylon bags, if you see the trade-marked name Cordura or Teflon (even better if the two are together), you know you're on the right track.

▲ Linings should always be stitched in, not glued on.

▲ Stitching should be double, with thick coated thread. Make certain that the finishing is done well, and that threads don't simply end or dangle.

▲ Handles are the pressure points of all bags, and a bag with a broken handle is far worse than no bag at all (it weighs more!).

On a cloth bag, canvas or nylon handles should be very apparently well sewn, with an X-shaped pattern to the stitching, and should never be sewn directly onto the material of the bag, but onto a thicker piece of material that helps distribute the pressure.

Plastic handles should be attached to hard luggage with rust-proof metal; check the inside of the bag to see if you can find where the handle is attached. If there's uncovered hardware there, you're going to end up with some snagged clothes.

If the choice is between leather and suede handles, always choose leather. And try to select a single-handled bag over a double-handled one, unless the two handles are held together by a snap-on piece: Porters often grab bags by just one handle, and if the bag's not

THE BAG	ADVANTAGES	DISADVANTAGES	PRICE RANGE
Louis Vuitton	Made of tough vinyl-impregnated canvas with leather trim; impeccably made; ages well; reasonably light; wide variety of shapes from steamer trunks on down	Very expensive; marks you as a wealthy traveler	$200–1250
Mark Cross leather	An ultimate luxury; well made; will last a lifetime with proper care; classic good styling	Requires a fair amount of care; pretty heavy; also see above	$575–650 (for pigskin and calf lines)
Aluminum hard-sided	Unquestionably chic	Unquestionably heavy	$400–600
Kelty	Handy, easily packable, sturdy; transforms into backpack for long hauls	Backpack addition adds some extra weight—unnecessary for short trips	$150–250
Hartmann top-of-the-line	One variety is tweedy, hard-wearing cloth with leather or suede trim; hard-sided and able to	Like other hard bags, requires special storage space; suede trim wears quickly; large pieces (as	$125–555

Lark top-of-the-line	Varieties include vinyl over canvas fabric, and rugged nylon; well-structured pieces will also expand slightly; resists dirt well	Not collapsible, so needs storage space; if vinyl on some pieces starts to peel, may be hard to repair	$75–300
Le Sportsac	The lightest luggage of all, in reinforced parachute nylon; great carry-on or weekender bag	Not recommended for all uses or serious travel (when bags must be checked); tends to attract dirt; canvas webbing handles may fray; ages poorly; very casual-looking	$45–120
L. L. Bean or Land's End canvas or Cordura nylon pieces	Sturdiest of the unstructured bags; can be packed very full; light and waterproof	Clothes inside bags often get same treatment as outside of bag; look is fairly casual; a large duffel version can be unwieldy	$25–75

constructed to hang all its weight from one handle, you
run the risk of having it—and its contents—damaged.
If the bag is at all large, look for handles that are
cushioned on the underside, to protect your hands.

▲ Check the quality of zippers by running them back and
forth several times to see that they work smoothly.
Again, look for double stitching and finished ends.

▲ Locks can't really help prevent theft (a knife is all that's
needed for soft-sided luggage), but they can be a deter-
rent. Most important, they help bags resist the temptation to pop open in transit. Look for recessed, built-in
locks on structured luggage. You can buy small
padlocks for your soft zippered bags; just make sure
there's a ring on the bag to which the end of the zipper
can be locked.

▲ Interior straps in hard and semi-soft suitcases are designed to hold clothes firmly when you open and close
a sectioned bag that opens in the middle. They also
help decrease wrinkling because they hold clothes in
place during transit. If your bag has them, use them.

▲ Built-in wheels sound like a great idea, but they sometimes don't work. Try out a suitcase with wheels in the
store, properly weighted as if full. When packed, a
large suitcase often has a mind of its own and will go in
the opposite direction from you and topple over—
very frustrating. When wheels are attached to the
short end of the suitcase, this effect can be even more
pronounced.

▲ About luggage carriers: We've all been impressed by

the sight of stewardesses sailing by with their suitcases rolling effortlessly behind on a luggage carrier. Are these carriers worthwhile? If you are a saleswoman, or if you must regularly pack more than you can comfortably carry, they can be a great help. Again, though, be sure you buy a quality product. Test one out in the store to make sure it is truly lightweight and collapses easily and quickly.

Tip: Regardless of how dirt- or water-resistant the fabric of the bag you select is claimed to be, it's a good idea to choose dark colors over light. That doesn't mean "decorator" avocado, either. Light colors simply show off dirt and smudges, and it sometimes seems as if airports have special devices for getting in a kind of dirt you just can't get out. Black is becoming quite popular, so if it suits your style, consider it seriously.

SIZING UP YOUR LUGGAGE NEEDS

Choosing the right luggage isn't just a question of fabric or construction. Weight, size, and style are crucial elements and may affect your choice of travel wardrobe more than you realize. Don't let a false sense of optimism guide you to choose luggage that's the wrong size for your needs.

Among the many warnings I can give you about packing a suitcase too full is the situation you might encounter during a stiff airport (customs or otherwise) inspection: If you thought it was hard work fitting all that stuff in before you finally got the suitcase to close in your bedroom, think of how tough it's going to be to repack on the floor at the airport. This is, of course, not to mention the fact that suitcases are more apt to split open when they've been stuffed.

What you're looking for is the balance between over-stuffed and just enough. We've seen the dangers of over-packing, while an underfilled bag can result in very wrinkled clothing. That's why you need to consider carefully your travel plans when shopping for the right bag. If necessary, sit down and make a list of the trips you've made in the past year. Write down the limitations of the bags you already own, to avoid repeating past mistakes. Think about what you want—visualize yourself on a trip—*then* go shopping for the bag.

Primarily business travel. If you're doing two- or three-day stints, and must wear suits, your best option will be a folding garment bag. These are not as bulky as they once were: There are triple-folded bags that end up the size of small suitcases, and don't hang down to below your knees. Garment bags have three important pluses: You can easily carry them yourself, since they come with a shoulder strap; they keep tailored clothes almost free of wrinkles; and you can carry them onto a plane with you. In addition, a useful garment bag will have individual zippered pockets—for a pair of shoes or two and for lingerie and a few folded items. You can also find versions of the garment bag with detachable cosmetics bags. This type of compartmentalized packing can be a great time-saver: You know precisely where everything is, and when the bag is hung on the back of a door, you've brought a closet along with you.

Week-long vacations. You'll want a bag that can handle just about anything, from beach towels to ragg wool sweaters. You'll want to look for a semi-soft nylon bag, in a medium size you know you can carry yourself.

All-purpose travel. The best advice is for you to invest in two bags from the same line (too many mixed pieces can give you a bag-lady look). One might be a garment bag and the other a soft-sided suitcase. This gives you a wide range of possibilities: A four-day trip should require only the small bag; a longer-than-one-week trip should require only the larger bag; both together should cover you for up to a month.

Tips: If you feel confident about traveling light, make that small suitcase an overnighter. Or, if the suitcase is reasonably thin, buy a shoulder strap to fit it. Your shoulder can usually carry more weight than your hands . . . and then they'll be free. If you have minimal storage space, look for bags that can nest inside one another when they're not being used, or collapsible soft luggage that can be stored flat.

The "everything" bag. Your most important bag, however, could well turn out to be what is sometimes called a flight bag (or overnighter, as mentioned above). This needs to be good-looking—you'll be carrying it often—and large enough to hold everything for a weekend trip or whatever you would need to keep with you during a flight (you'll get the rundown on contents in the next chapter on packing), but small enough to fit into an overhead carrier or under the seat on a plane. One of the best and most versatile bags around is the Danish schoolbag (or Souperbag). Its rectangular shape is classic, and its thick shoulder strap is strong and comfortable. Best of all is the fact that it is truly expandable—it has a zipper all around the edge that, when undone, effectively doubles the amount of space you've got to work with. Its shape easily accommodates books and papers, a change of clothes, and cosmetics and other necessities. The numerous compartments make finding things a snap. This particular bag is canvas (and unfortunately *you* will need to waterproof it) and comes in a myriad of colors and costs about $60. It's available from The Chocolate Soup, 946 Madison Avenue, New York, NY 10021 (212-861-2210).

But whatever bag you choose for your "everything" bag, make sure it has a comfortable shoulder strap, is well constructed in general, and is a neutral color (gray, brown, black).

The bag you'll never need. Take the hard-sided cosmetics case with the mirror in the top, fill it with the old cosmetic potions you've rooted from your medicine chest, and give it to some deserving child. You'll never travel light with one of those! Instead, you should use a compact plastic or plastic-lined cosmetics bag. These days, you can find bags in every size, color, and price range imaginable. But you should keep in mind the fact that spills are inevitable at some point, and for that reason, I think it's best to go with cheaper bags that you won't feel bad about discarding. Besides, it's fun to shop for a new one as a treat before you go on a trip. Most large five-and-dimes have a good selection of clear plastic zippered bags for a minimal outlay of cash. As long as you're at the store, shop for travel-sized necessities, as well as for the small empty plastic bottles and jars you'll need to transfer other potions you can't find in prepackaged small sizes.

The "extra" bag. Don't forget to pack a sturdy, foldable tote bag whenever you travel for longer than a weekend (or whenever you're going to a big city). The material should be thin but strong—parachute nylon is an excellent choice. You can fit it into your handbag when you go sightseeing—it makes shopping that much easier. You can put all your purchases in it when you leave to make passage through customs quicker: Everything will be in one place.

Tip: Leaving college behind doesn't mean you have to forget its good ideas. Remember backpacks? While I'm not necessarily suggesting that you pack all your belong-

ings in the big metal-frame sort, a scaled-down model—
the knapsack—can be a lifesaver. If you're on a casual
vacation, it can be just the ticket for day trips from your
hotel (when you need to carry a sweater, a guidebook,
camera, maybe a change of shoes so you can go directly to
dinner) or for shopping expeditions. Your hands remain
free, and a fine specimen costs only about $20–30.

THE CARE AND FEEDING OF LUGGAGE

Since you've made an investment in good quality luggage,
you'll want to take good care of it to prolong its life. Save
the directions that come with the bags; they'll tell you
what your particular bags need. It's also a good idea to ask
the dealer for his recommendations.

Repairs should be made as soon as you discover a
problem. If not, you're likely to forget about it until you
start to pack for another trip. If you suspect that damage
is due to a fault in the bag itself, don't hesitate to contact
the manufacturer, who will often repair for free if this is
the case. Damaged locks, handles, and hinges can usually
be fixed, but you should be certain you're dealing with a
reputable repairman.

Leather luggage demands the most consistent care. It's
a good idea to use only the type of cleaning and oiling
products specified for the bag by the manufacturer. Vinyl
and urethane bags can simply be wiped clean with a damp
cloth and mild soap. The interior of hard luggage can be

cleaned of dust with a vacuum cleaner, and wiped with a cloth. If you've used water, make sure you leave the bag open long enough to let it dry thoroughly, to avoid mildew. Store your bags in a dry place, covered loosely with plastic. Unless your attic is well insulated, the extremes of temperature usually found there make it unsuitable for any type of luggage. Find someplace that is more or less consistently at room temperature.

4 Pack, Get Set, Go!

*P*acking can be quite an art, as you already know if you've never quite gotten it right. But to travel light—which includes arriving with unmussed clothing—you need to pack like a pro. Use this chapter as a guide to wrinkle- and hassle-free packing.

Traveling light isn't only about weight and size. It's about convenience too. Besides the fact that you'll be spared having to dump the entire contents of your suitcase out onto the hotel bed in search of the skirt you think you may have brought, careful packing can save you time and trouble on the way.

SOME PRELIMINARY WORDS OF CAUTION

One of the greatest benefits of really traveling light is minimizing the possibility that your baggage will be lost or damaged by careless handlers. If you're making a simple one-destination week-or-under trip by plane, you should be able to carry everything with you onto the plane (in soft luggage). That's the only way to be certain that your bags make it all the way with you and in one piece. To do this, you need to divide your belongings into two more or less evenly weighted carry-ons, in the manner described below. (The list is general; you'll think of other things you'll need depending on the specifics of the trip.) You'll find, too, that it's far easier to carry two similar bags, one on either side for balance, than one large and one small. Your shoulder bag should go under the seat in front of you on the plane, the other in the overhead compartment.

SHOULDER BAG	SUITCASE OR HANGING BAG
jewelry	clothing
important papers	shoes
money	lingerie
camera, travel clock	handbags
small appliances	accessories (other than jewelry)
books, magazines	folding umbrella
cosmetics, medications	extra tote bag or knapsack
cardigan sweater	raincoat (if not worn)

You'll have everything you need, and everything of great value, right in front of your eyes at all times. And, if worse comes to worst, you could check the clothing bag through if you were directed to do so. But the best is that when you leave the plane, you can leave the airport immediately—and avoid the seemingly endless wait at the baggage carousel. The discipline it takes to pare the packing list is amply rewarded by the freedom and safety gained.

Tip: Here's a basic rule of thumb: For weekend or overnight trips, a bag 14″ by 22″ should do; for a week-long trip, one 19″ by 27″ ("standard" size); for a two-week trip, both should carry all your needs.

LABELING YOUR LUGGAGE

Lost luggage is no joke, nor is it an impossibility. Though it is rarely lost forever, it is frequently lost at the most inopportune times (like the beginning of vacation, not when you get home). You have no choice but to check bulky items like skis, or a large number of bags (if you're going abroad for a number of months).

Still, checking luggage always involves risk. A friend of mine once arrived in Greece for a six-month stay via a tortuous route that landed her first in New York, then Switzerland, then Italy, and finally Athens. The bags didn't make it that far. After two weeks of waiting (and complaining on a daily basis to the airlines office) the bags were located in a Rome police station. Miraculously, they each arrived in one piece, though all were soaking wet (remember what I said about waterproof bags?).

Thousands upon thousands of people annually complain about mishandled luggage. The more frequently you travel, the more you risk having your bags delayed, damaged, or lost. If you can't avoid checking luggage through on an airplane, train, or bus, there are a few things you should know about to try to make certain your bags arrive when you do, and in the same condition as when you checked them.

▲ Make sure your bags are clearly identified with your name. Attach an identification tag to the outside of the case, and put your name on the inside as well, along with a copy of your itinerary. Use a business rather than a home address. Thieves often scout the departure lines at airports, and know just where to go when they read your home address.

▲ Never check luggage that is damaged or unlocked. The chances are that you'll get it back in worse condition than when you checked it—and important items may be missing completely.

▲ Although they may have sentimental value, remove previous airport tags to avoid confusion among the handlers as to where your luggage is going this trip.

▲ Watch the ticket agent as he/she attaches the airport destination tag to your bag. If you're not certain that it's the right tag, ask. Wait to see the agent place your bag on the appropriate conveyor belt. Luggage can be delayed if the agent gets sidetracked.

▲ Get to the airport with lots of time to spare. In peak traveling times, like holidays, this means an hour ahead of departure for domestic flights, and one and a half to two hours for overseas trips.

▲ If what you're carrying is particularly valuable, do consider extra insurance. The airline's liability, described on your ticket, may very well not begin to include what you're checked. Check to see if tickets purchased with your credit card carry additional trip coverage.

▲ *Never* check important papers, jewelry, money, or medicine. These items are never covered by insurance, and their loss can cause great problems even if your luggage is only delayed.

▲ To make retrieval at the baggage claim easier, consider wrapping the handle of your suitcase with brightly colored plastic tape. It will leap to your attention the moment it enters the carousel.

If the worst happens, and your bags don't appear, or they come through minus some important element, go directly to the baggage office near the carousels. You'll have to fill out forms, and even argue a bit (nicely, of course!), but you should get some response. If you receive a settlement check later that doesn't agree with your assessment of the situation, don't cash the check, but pursue the issue further with the airline.

PACKING IT IN

If you've followed the suggestions in chapter 1, your clothing, accessories, and cosmetics are all ready to go. Now the question is: what to bring? First, think about the purpose of your trip and your destination.

If you're traveling on business, you need to consider the impression you want to make. No matter how bright and adept you are, if you don't appear to care about how you look or seem to appreciate the importance of details, it will be hard to convince your clients that you will do a good job for them. So it's not only the condition of your clothing that matters, but its appropriateness. Reread the wardrobe chapter here, and give yourself a good, hard look in the mirror. A tight jersey dress on a body that is anything less than model-perfect can, unfortunately, get looks of the sort you can't risk at a business appointment.

If you're going on vacation, think about what sort it will be, what you plan to do, and what the weather will be. Will you need dressy clothes as well as casual wear? Will you be doing any sports? Sightseeing? I think you get the picture—on to packing it in!

The best way to make the final decisions about your travel wardrobe is to gather all the items you want to bring and lay them out on your bed. Make sure the lighting is good, so that you can match colors exactly. Lay out single outfits with all their transforming accessories in the proper places to make sure they'll work. Ask yourself, for instance, if that belt goes well with the slacks and the simple dress, and if your dressy sandals look good with the same dress and the shawl you plan to wear with it at night. If there's an outfit you haven't yet tried on together, now is the time to do it.

To a certain degree, you must let the size of the bag (the smallest one you could logically use) determine how much you're going to bring. Unless you're certain you've already pared down to the essentials, there is usually at least one thing you could do without.

If your destination is a warm climate, have on hand a pile of tissue paper sheets; if you're going someplace cold, use dry cleaners' plastic bags. When you pack around these fillers, they create air pockets among your clothes to keep them from wrinkling.

Begin by placing heavy items—shoes, handbags, books—on the bottom of a suitcase at the hinged side (so they'll already be at the bottom when gravity exerts its force). Fill your shoes with socks, rolled underwear, belts, and other small items. This uses every bit of available space, while it helps shoes keep their shape. Do the same with your handbag or clutch. Shoes should then be placed inside untied plastic bags (so that the leather can breathe a bit) or covered with old socks. Position high heels in the case so that the heels point inwards—important in every kind of bag, except perhaps hard-sided luggage.

After you've buttoned and zipped them, encase single items of clothing inside the plastic bags or on top of a sheet or two of tissue paper. Then, depending on the kind of bag you use, follow these directions:

In a hard or semi-soft suitcase: With tailored, non-jersey clothes, use this "interfolding" technique. You'll avoid the sharp creases that result when you fold each piece separately. When you unpack, you'll see only gentle folds that won't show badly at all.

Starting with the most delicate piece, place one half inside the bag, draping the other half outside. Place another item on top, draping half outside the bag on the opposite side from the first item (see page 116). Keep alternating items of clothing until all are half in/half out, on both sides. Then, still alternating sides, fold them into the bag, one over another, so that one half of each article is folded on top of another. Fill in empty space around the edges with smaller, folded items (like lingerie) or balls of tissue paper. Use garment straps, if your bag has them.

In a garment bag: If your bag has separate pockets, use them for shoes. If not, place them in plastic bags at the bottom of the bag. Enclose hanging clothes in plastic bags.

In soft luggage: All jersey and casual clothing can be rolled (around tissue or plastic) and laid side by side over heavier items like shoes. Delicate or tailored pieces should go on top, with as few folds as possible. Cover everything with a layer of plastic.

WHEN YOU ARRIVE

As soon as possible after you arrive at your destination, you should unpack, even if it means only hanging your

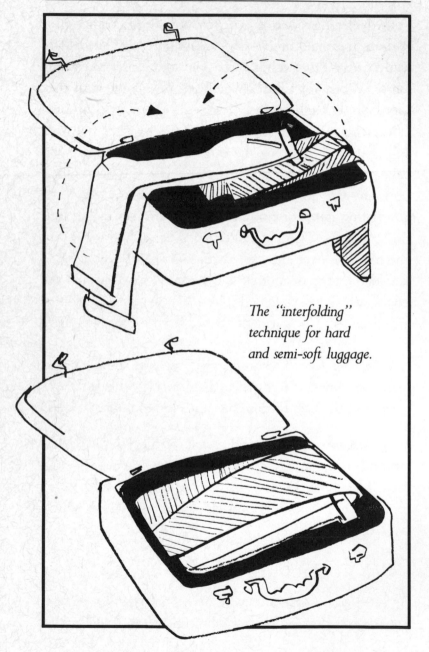

The "interfolding"
technique for hard
and semi-soft luggage.

clothes over the back of a chair. If you're placing clothes in drawers, refold them so luggage creases aren't further reinforced. Hang any wrinkled items in the bathroom and run a hot shower (whether you take it or not) with the door closed. Ten to fifteen minutes in a steamy bathroom should remove most wrinkles.

5 On Your Way

NEGOTIATING THE AIRPORT AND THE FLIGHT

*T*here's no doubt about it: We're going faster and farther than ever, all thanks to the airplane. And because the competition for travelers is pretty fierce, the airlines are always thinking up new ways to attract customers. Usually, you're the beneficiary of these added treats, which range from reduced fares and frequent-traveler bonuses to more exciting food and other in-flight extras. Still, negotiating the airport and getting through the flight unscathed takes some know-how. In this chapter, you'll find flying-color tips—most of which are also applicable to other modes of travel.

You should always read your airline ticket carefully
before your trip, down to the small print—even if you
think you know what it says. It's especially important to
know your rights and the airline's restrictions now that
the industry is increasingly less regulated.

If you're going to be carrying odd-sized, fragile, or
valuable packages, you should phone the carrier to learn
about their rules and liabilities; each airline is slightly
different. You will also always have certain rights regard-
ing lost, damaged, or delayed baggage, but it's important
to know the extent of those rights *before* you hand your
possessions over. Finally, you should be well versed in
what your personal insurance covers while you're traveling; if you find you need additional coverage for a trip,
talk to your travel agent (remember how important I told
you he/she can be?) about your specific requirements.

The first step of flying hassle-free is getting to the airport
with enough time—but not too much—to assure that
your bags get on the plane (if you're traveling heavy
enough to warrant check-through), as well as to make
sure you're not one of the latecomers who gets bumped
from the frequently overbooked flights. Early arrival also
increases your chance of getting a choice seat in the
location you prefer. Although you always have a right to a
seat in the non-smoking section, you could have (and
cause) some problems if you check in as the plane is
boarding and the only remaining seat is in a smoking
section. Other popular seating choices go fast too: win-

dow seats (for the view) and aisle seats (for those precious extra inches of legroom). And if you want to sit in the most stable part of the plane, get there early to request a seat in the midsection, over the forward part of the plane.

Tip: Most airlines can arrange advance seat selection when you purchase your ticket. This option can save you time and irritation and is well worth asking about.

If you have any reason to anticipate a problem—bad weather, holiday crowding—do call the airport before you leave home to make sure your flight hasn't been delayed. If there's no way to avoid a long wait, you have at least one option, beyond buying a chocolate bar and a magazine or book and settling in for some wasted hours.

Most major airlines (including United, Eastern, TWA, and American, among others) have special clubs you can join for a yearly fee. Their own lounges, located in most large airports, can be a real treat for the woman traveler: The privacy and clubby atmosphere will probably make you feel much more comfortable than the hubbub and dinginess of the regular airport cocktail lounge. What's more, the hostess has up-to-the-minute departure information, you can make your seat selection from the club, and you can often use the club phone to make local social or business calls while sipping free coffee. These clubs often prove to be worth more than the membership fee, especially when you have a lengthy layover. And if you travel frequently for your job, this membership might be covered by your employer, and if not, can be tax-deductible.

When you finally do make it onto the plane, you'll begin to realize the extent to which the airlines clamor for your business. Here are a few of the things a tourist or economy-class passenger can expect:

▲ Special meals. These need to be ordered at least twenty-four hours in advance, or when you order your ticket, but are often a lovely change of pace. At last, you don't need to eat what they give everyone else! You can get vegetarian, kosher, no-salt, low-cholesterol, and many other types of meals. I won't vouch for the quality of all of them, but they are often tastier and healthier than the regular airplane meal. Ask for specifics when you phone the ticketing office.

   Whichever meal you choose, it's a good idea to eat lightly while in the air; it can help reduce the effects of jet lag and the bloated feeling you often feel at high altitudes.

▲ Freebies. Of course, you know about the in-flight magazine (which may be worth a look). But did you know that in the bathroom you'll often find sanitary napkins? (Tampons are harder to find.) The flight attendant can also provide you with playing cards, a packet of writing paper and envelopes, and aspirin. On longer flights you can usually get a sleep mask and slippers and even toiletry kits to keep, in addition to the pillow and blanket the airlines lend for the duration of the flight. Individual airlines sometimes have their own gimmicks: hot towels, free newspapers, free wine tastings. Take advantage!

To help make the trip as comfortable as possible, wear loose-fitting clothes. Sitting on a plane for a few hours can make your legs and feet swell, so be sure to wear comfortable (read *roomy*)—shoes, and avoid wearing boots if at all possible. To counteract some of the effects of being at high altitude, drink plenty of fluids, such as juice and water. Unfortunately, alcohol can really do a number on you in the air—its dehydrating and intoxicating effects are stronger in the air than on the ground—so take it easy.

Tip: If you wear contact lenses, take them out before you fly. It can be uncomfortable to doze with them in your eyes, and dry cabin air can make your eyes feel scratchy if you leave your lenses in. Everyone will find soothing eye drops handy to have on board.

Speaking of dryness, an absolute must is a tube of skin moisturizer, which should be stowed in your flight bag. You can actually see what the dry cabin air can do to your skin in a very short while if you look in a mirror. If your skin isn't treated to frequent applications of a good lotion, you will probably see white flecks of dry skin on your face. Your lips may get chapped quickly, too.

For this reason, it's wise to wear only minimal makeup when you're on the plane. When you hear the announcement that the plane is making its approach to your destination, slip off to the bathroom to ready yourself for *your* final approach.

If you've got some time on your hands in the plane (as you undoubtedly do!) and don't feel like reading, you can do yourself a favor by exercising. It's important to initiate some movement every now and again to avoid feeling sluggish. Just getting up to take a few turns around the plane can help get blood to circulate. If you're fairly uninhibited, stand up in the aisle and stretch. If you don't want to advertise yourself, though, there's plenty to do in your seat.

While seated, with back straight:

1. Lift one knee straight up about 8", exhaling as you do; then, while inhaling, slowly return leg to sitting position. Repeat eight times for each leg.

2. Simultaneously grasp both wrists with opposite hands, in brief, strong holds. Tighten muscles, hold, relax. Keep elbows pointed away from body at right angles. Do eight times; rest; repeat.

3. Lift both shoulders up toward ears and inhale; drop them and exhale. Do eight times.

4. Gradually bend head sideways (ear to shoulder) as you keep looking straight ahead and exhale; inhale as

you slowly straighten back up. Do eight times to each side.

While standing against a wall (rear of plane is best), with feet apart:

1. Rise up on balls of feet, then slowly return to a full stand; bend knees, keeping heels flat on the floor, then slowly return to stand. Repeat entire sequence sixteen times.

2. Lean forward on balls of feet and let your torso, head, and arms hang loosely forward, with your hands dangling in front of your feet; hang there with knees slightly bent for one minute, then "roll" back up to stand.

3. Look at the ceiling as you alternately stretch each arm above your head. Do sixteen times with each arm.

If you do all of these exercises, you will have worked almost every muscle group in your body. You will find other exercises suitable for a plane trip on page 130.

It's not a bad idea to concentrate on your posture as well. Let your shoulders drop—relax them completely—and you may find you've been scrunching them up needlessly. Sit up straight!

Finally, remember that you're a captive for a while. So, if you don't have work that needs immediate attention, grit your teeth and pull out a calculator and your checkbook. It'll be just one more thing that will be balanced when you get off the plane!

We've saved the unfortunate worst for last: jet lag. It is quite literally a drag. Just when you're faced with a whole new world of sights to see, you may find yourself simply too weary to cope. Worse, you may feel disoriented, or you may lose your concentration quickly. Your whole system, including your digestion, can get off kilter.

It's important not to schedule many activities or meet- ings for your first day after a long flight. Give yourself time to get acclimated. But there's more you can do to prevent the effects of jet lag: Research has shown that if you regulate your diet for about three days before you fly overseas—one day eating greater amounts of protein and carbohydrates, and eating sparingly the next day—you can help your body accept the time-zone changes more easily. The Anti-Jet-Lag Diet on page 126 was developed by Charles Ehret of the Argonne National Laboratory. If you'd like your own copy of the diet on a wallet-sized card, send a self-addressed, stamped envelope to Argonne National Laboratory, 9700 South Cass Avenue, Argonne, IL 60439.

OTHER WAYS OF GOING

Just because more and more of us are taking to the air doesn't mean we aren't using other transportation, too. For many, the vehicle of choice or necessity is the car.

How to avoid jet lag:

1. **DETERMINE BREAKFAST TIME** at destination on day of arrival.

2. **FEAST-FAST-FEAST-FAST** on home time. Start three days before departure day. On day one, FEAST, eat heartily with high-protein breakfast and lunch and a high-carbohydrate dinner. No coffee except between 3 and 5 p.m. On day two, FAST on light meals of salads, light soups, fruits and juices. Again, no coffee except between 3 and 5 p.m. On day three, FEAST again. On day four, departure day, FAST; if you drink caffeinated beverages, take them in morning when traveling west, or between 6 and 11 p.m. when traveling east. Going west, you may fast only half day.

3. **BREAK FINAL FAST** at destination breakfast time. No alcohol on plane. If flight is long enough, sleep until normal breakfast time at destination, *but no later.* Wake up and FEAST on high-protein breakfast. Stay awake, active. Continue day's meals according to meal times at destination.

COUNTDOWN

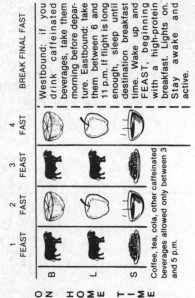

	1 FEAST	2 FAST	3 FEAST	4 FAST	BREAK FINAL FAST
B					Westbound: if you drink caffeinated beverages, take them morning before departure. Eastbound: take them between 6 and 11 p.m. If flight is long enough, sleep until destination breakfast time. Wake up and FEAST, beginning with a high-protein breakfast. Lights on. Stay awake and active.
O N E L					
T I M E S					

Coffee, tea, cola, other caffeinated beverages allowed only between 3 and 5 p.m.

ARGONNE NATIONAL LABORATORY
ANTI-JET-LAG DIET

The Argonne Anti-Jet-Lag Diet is helping travelers quickly adjust their bodies' internal clocks to new time zones. It is also being used to speed the adjustment of shiftworkers, such as power plant operators, to periodically rotating work hours. The diet was developed by Dr. Charles F. Ehret of Argonne's Division of Biological and Medical Research as an application of his fundamental studies of the daily biological rhythms of animals. Argonne National Laboratory is one of the U. S. Department of Energy's major centers of research in energy and the fundamental sciences. Argonne National Laboratory, 9700 South Cass Avenue, Argonne, Illinois 60439

FEAST on high protein breakfasts and lunches to stimulate the body's active cycle. Suitable meals include steak, eggs, hamburgers, high-protein cereals, green beans.

FEAST on high-carbohydrate suppers to stimulate sleep. They include spaghetti and other pastas (but no meatballs), crepes (but no meat filling), potatoes, other starchy vegetables, and sweet desserts.

FAST days help deplete the liver's store of carbohydrates and prepare the body's clock for resetting. Suitable foods include fruit, light soups, broths, skimpy salads, unbuttered toast, half pieces of bread. Keep calories and carbohydrates to a minimum.

And train and bus companies are beefing up service and making it possible to glide ever more easily between metropolitan centers. Cruises are on the rise too: A greater variety is available, including more cruises that appeal to women traveling alone. So take these suggestions to heart!

By car. Don't get carried away by the fact that you've got plenty of room in a car. First of all, the temptation to bring too much without careful planning can lead to the same problems in a car jaunt as in an airplane trip: a lot of confusion, and the possibility that with all that stuff, nothing will go together properly. Second, overloading can affect the way your car handles. Third, luggage racks on top of a car create wind resistance, which cuts fuel efficiency. So think twice before using them. If you *do* need luggage and bike racks (as you might for a summer trip to the beach), they can be rented as well as bought.

Another thing to remember is that you will need to bring everything that you can't store in a locked trunk into the motel at night—a car full of suitcases is an open invitation to a thief. If you stop somewhere different every night, this can be quite a hassle.

▲ If you're taking any sort of road trip, it's a great idea to join a motor club before you leave. Two of the best known and most widely available are the Motor Club of America and, of course, "Triple A" (American Automobile Association). Both can prove to be lifesavers, as

they provide services from emergency towing to advice
and maps to start your trip. (AAA has terrific "Triptik"
maps which show the best route for you in detailed
sections, all spiral-bound for easy reading.)

▲ If you're planning to drive while abroad, you may need
an international driving permit. You can apply for one
at an AAA office.

▲ Make sure your car has the proper emergency equipment: jumper cables, spare tire, jack, white flag (for
breakdowns), ice scraper, wrench, first aid kit, anti-
freeze solution, flares, blanket, and flashlight.

▲ If you're driving in the summer, do wear loose and
cool clothing (all-cotton is best). Jersey fabric won't get
as wrinkled as plain cotton in the heat.

▲ If your car has vinyl seats, avoid wearing shorts—you
can really burn your legs after the car's been parked in
the sun. Two ideas to avoid the "hot seat": Keep a
towel handy to place on the seat, or buy a woven-
straw seat cover.

▲ Driving shoes are both fun and practical for long
drives: They can save you from blisters on your heels,
and they have a rubber bottom that won't slip off
pedals. Bernardo makes one style, and L. L. Bean car-
ries its own brand.

▲ Good sunglasses are absolutely essential!

▲ The automotive section of a large variety store is bound
to have some items that can be very useful: a specially
designed drinking cup with a base that sticks to the
dashboard; a coin dispenser that keeps coin denomina-

tions separate and at your fingertips when you need them for tolls; a small wastebasket for the floor.

▲ Car trips provide a perfect opportunity for you to get exercise along the way. Pack your lunch in a Styrofoam ice chest, and take a small detour in pretty countryside. Get out of the car, breathe deeply, and run around! You need to keep your blood moving in order to stay alert.

▲ Remember that although car windows keep out the burning rays of the sun, an *open* window doesn't. I've seen people with very red left arms after driving with one arm against the window sill. Keep some sunscreen handy and use it liberally.

▲ Don't push yourself while driving—it can be dangerous. Eight or ten hours at a stretch is the most anyone can expect to do and still remain awake. If you must drive longer, or if you find yourself getting drowsy, stop, have some coffee, and do some jumping jacks. Lean over and let the blood return to your head. Keep some gum or hard candy at hand to keep your mouth, and you, awake.

▲ I know I hardly need to say it, but watch out for local speed limits and parking regulations. It's no fun to get speeding tickets, to leave a cozy little park to find your car's been towed, or to find out the hard way that right turn on red is not permitted.

By bus. If you're traveling overland in the US, you might want to consider taking a bus instead of driving yourself.

Buses can be comfortable for shorter distances; they afford you the freedom to look at the scenery, and take the pressure off you and your car. Of course, you don't have the option to stop wherever you like, but a bus can keep going when you wouldn't be able to. Bus travel is also reasonably priced, and buses are air-conditioned and usually have bathrooms.

▲ To avoid feeling logy, you can do exercises in a bus as well as in a plane. Here are some good (and quiet) exercises to try:

1. Jogging on the spot: Sitting upright, let your upper thighs do the work as you simulate a quick run in place.

2. Shoulder roll: Roll both shoulders forward in a circular motion five times; reverse direction. You can alternate this one with other exercises; it's a great relaxer, too.

3. Ankle roll: If there's space, stretch your legs out below the seat in front of you. With your toes pointed, circle your feet in alternating directions. Then repeat with flexed feet.

4. Buttocks squeeze: This one is practically imperceptible. Tighten your bottom muscles (and your thighs too) until you feel yourself rise a bit in your seat. Hold for a count of five, then relax. Repeat four times.

▲ You should bring along some food, enough for an initial picnic (and a little extra—bus-trippers invariably make friends). Bread, fruit, granola bars, and dried fruit and nuts (non-messy foods) are good and healthy. If you're counting calories, you can bring carrot sticks, fruit, and packaged Melba toast. The new "soft packs" of juice are ideal for travelers.

▲ Don't sit in the last few rows unless you're an avid smoker. The bathroom is in the back of the bus too, so avoid this high-traffic area.

▲ Dress comfortably, of course. Do make sure you've got a sweater with you, as the air conditioning can make it chilly.

▲ Tuck into your bag a few pre-moistened paper tow-elettes or a small spritz-bottle of mineral water, for a quick morning facial refresher.

By train. The wonderful thing about trains is that they can literally be hotels on wheels. The extra price you pay for a little room (a couchette—there are different grades and sizes available) is well worth it, if your journey is an overnight one. You can cover many miles while asleep. You can, for instance, board an Amtrak train in New York in the evening, have a drink, a chat, time for reading, enjoy a sound night's sleep in a full-size bed, and wake up well rested and refreshed in Toronto the next morning.

▲ Pack all your necessities, including a nightgown and a change of clothes, in a small bag that's easier and quicker to open and close than your large suitcase, if you've had to bring one.

▲ In a couchette, you can do almost any exercise the space will allow. For an overnight train trip, you might want to bring a "personal stereo" along with some exercise tapes or music tapes to dance to. Trains are also great places to get work done. Even if you don't have your own little room, train seats are usually roomy and steady enough to allow writing and reading. If you feel isolated, you can always take a trip to the bar car, where the atmosphere may be quite friendly.

On a cruise. Be sure to talk to your travel agent about the specifics of your trip, but here are some tips to get you going on a smooth sail.

▲ Extra baggage insurance is almost always a necessity, as the cruise line will only take minimal responsibility— as little as $100 per person. That's very little in any case, but considering that you are sometimes allowed to bring on board as much as 200 pounds of luggage, it may not even be enough to cover your lingerie!

▲ On a seven-day cruise, you need at least two "fancy" outfits for evening cocktails and dinner. On many cruises, however, you won't need to "dress" every night. You can get dress information before you go from your travel agent.

▲ Cruise ships these days are veritable floating health clubs, so be sure to bring sportswear for the things you like to do.

▲ Read the material the cruise line sends you. There may be a costume party planned, in which case you might want to tuck away an extra accessory or two, like a gypsy scarf or elegant demi-mask.

▲ If you're on a special diet, you'll probably be able to order special meals on board. Have your travel agent check into this in advance.

▲ More often than not, although you may use electric shavers and hair dryers in your room, you can't use travel irons. (Their power requirements can overload a ship's electric capacity.) That's why easy-care clothes are particularly recommended. Laundry service is generally available, but extravagantly expensive, so you'll save money if you can so some washing by hand yourself.

▲ These days, the dress code on board ship is likely to be more flexible than before. If you want to bring along some of your best dresses, don't hesitate to do so, especially if the cruise is the only part of your vacation: You can take much more than if you were hopping on and off planes. The ship's newspaper will tell you the appropriate dress for each night.

▲ You might consider getting a new bathing suit or two if your prime activity will be sunning and swimming on deck. Choose simple maillots that will look great with a pareo tied in skirt fashion at the hips—a look that can take you from poolside to supper on deck in no time.

▲ If you're traveling alone and would like to meet people, ask the dining room steward to seat you at a large table.

▲ Choose the second meal seating—if you'd like to avoid eating with children and elderly couples.

▲ About tipping: It's customary to tip once a week the people who most often attend to your needs, such as dining room personnel, your maid, and the pool attendant—but never ship's officers. Enclose the tip in a white envelope with the recipient's name on it. The exact amount of each tip can be a delicate matter, but here are some guidelines: cabin crew, $4 each per day; dining room steward, $3 per day; maître d', $15–25 total; sommelier, 15% of your total wine bill; steward, $7 per day (with instructions to share with other stateroom personnel). On smaller boats where each crew member does several duties, you may be able to pay a simple 10% of the total cruise price to be divvied up by all. At any rate, when in doubt, you can always ask the purser what's appropriate.

▲ Longer cruises attract older people; up to seven days is usually more appealing to younger people.

6 Traveling Abroad

*T*raveling abroad takes special planning, but it needn't be a trip into the unknown. A good, knowledgeable travel agent can make your travel arrangements easy and advise you on medical, insurance, and other matters for your particular trip. Some guidelines are included here.

HEALTH

One of your first concerns should be preserving your health. Malaria, hepatitis, typhoid, cholera, and yellow fever in some areas requires vaccination and/or prophylactic measures. Ask your travel agent or the airline what shots or preparations are advised, and confer with your doctor. Be sure to get, and bring with you, an International Certificate of Vaccination, as well as copies of all prescriptions you are on. It's a good idea to know the generic names of any prescription drugs you take, too, as it may be difficult to find the identical medication abroad. If you're planning a long trip, ask your doctor to fill out a medical record for you to take along. If you wear eyeglasses or contact lenses, bring along an extra set as well as the prescription; replacing them may be difficult.

Certain countries can prove disastrous if you're not careful. Mexico, India, and South American countries seem to be prime offenders in terms of "Montezuma's Revenge" (or "Delhi Belly"). Your doctor can recommend nonprescription (Pepto-Bismol) or prescription (Lomotil) medications, but you can help stave off an attack with the following suggestions:

▲ Exercise a bit of caution about where you eat. Ask around, and avoid places where the tableware is chipped (that's where those nasty germs breed) or dirty, or where the waiters don't look absolutely clean. Unclean hands and utensils are a major problem.

▲ Think twice about eating any uncooked food, including salads and fruits. If you're cooking for yourself, give anything raw a particularly good scrub in clean (and preferably bottled or boiled) water. To be extra certain, peel all fruit.

▲ Some travelers have found that acidophilus capsules

(available in health food stores) are a good preventive measure, as they coat the stomach to ward off upsets.

▲ Stay away from food you suspect may have been re-heated. All meat should be thoroughly cooked.

▲ In many countries the milk that is available is un-pasteurized. Need I say more than that? Most cheese, however, is probably OK.

▲ Tap water may or may not be unclean. To be sure, however, you can usually buy bottled water or soda—but stay away from local brands and go for names you know. Arm yourself before you leave with water purification tablets. They can be a bother, but in a pinch you should use them.

▲ If everything fails and you begin to suffer, take the Lomotil or other medication you brought, but for no more than three or four days. If you're still suffering after that—or at any time, if there's blood in your stool—see a doctor.

Strangely enough, the opposite affliction can be a big problem for overseas travelers, too. Constipation is probably due to the upsetting of the normal routine (often an adjunct of jet lag), or to not drinking enough fluids. To help ease the problem, make sure you drink enough (clean) water, and do give yourself time over breakfast. If you're prone to this sort of thing, and if you take something for it, bring your own medication from home, because what you find abroad is not necessarily familiar (and what you need is often difficult to describe to a local pharmacist!). But don't dose yourself immediately upon arrival: The cure can be worse than the affliction.

One world traveler I know takes a package of miller's bran (found in health food stores) wherever she goes. Two teaspoons a day, she swears, keeps her perfectly regular regardless of any other symptoms of jet lag she might suffer. She also recommends lemon juice and hot water as an everyday breakfast drink, for the same reason.

Here is a basic list of medical supplies you may want to take on a trip abroad. Consult your doctor about which you're likely to need, and be sure you have a suitable supply.

any medications you normally take (including oral
  contraceptives)
medication for ailments you might be prone to (like
  vaginitis)
antimalarial drug (if indicated)
aspirin
Lomotil or similar (available by prescription)
calamine lotion
antiseptic cream
antifungal ointment
adhesive bandages in various sizes
sunscreen
insect repellent
laxative
thermometer

Dramamine or similar (against motion sickness)

vitamins (especially vitamin C for warding off colds)

Tip: If your destination is five or more thousand feet above sea level, plan on taking the first day or two easy. Until you're used to the high altitude, you may suffer from mild headaches or dizziness. If you're going to a ski resort, for instance, don't try to go out to the slopes immediately. The better your overall physical condition, though, the less adversely affected you'll be.

SAFETY

You also need to be more alert than usual for your own safety when traveling abroad. Apart from being easily identifiable as a tourist in most cases, a woman is frequently considered an easy mark for things like verbal abuse, pickpocketing, or worse. Unfortunately, you should be wary of someone who seems overly friendly or helpful. Be kind, but keep your distance until you're certain the motives are spotless. Here are a few other precautions you should take:

▲ Write down the name and address of your hotel, and keep it with you when you venture out.

▲ Ask the concierge or someone at the hotel desk how to describe, in simple terms, the location of your hotel (including cross streets and landmarks). Be sure you

state it clearly to cab drivers, so they're not tempted to
show you the scenic route.

▲ Your consular office can't help you out of all scrapes,
but it can be of enormous help if you've lost your
passport, or if you need help with a money transfer
from the US. The office also has lists of English-speak-
ing doctors.

▲ You've no doubt been cautioned many times never to
leave money or valuables in a hotel room, and that's
solid advice. But what to do if a hotel safe isn't available? The obvious solution, of course, has always been a
money belt. But, if like many women, you find them
uncomfortable or too bulky, you can always try a
special pouch (available by mail order and in travel
shops) designed to be attached across the chest to your
bra straps. Or you could securely pin a cloth pouch to
the inner waistband of pants or skirt. My own favorite
solution, though, is the classic photographer's vest: All
those snapped and zippered pockets not only carry
valuables safely, but a well-made khaki version lends
safari-style flair to a casual outfit of the type you'd wear
in rugged terrain, hiking, or anywhere dressing up is
not a priority.

MONEY

Finally, money matters, customs, and currency regulations are definitely more complex when you leave the US.
So it's important to learn the basics from your travel

agent and/or a good guidebook *before* you arrive overseas.
Here are some preliminary tips on currency:

▲ You've undoubtedly heard it said before, but it bears
repeating: Be sure you leave home with enough currency of the country of your destination to cover a
contingency or two: a cab ride, porters' tips, a snack.
However, keep the amount to a minimum, and instead
change a bit more at the airport on arrival in the
country, where the exchange rate is bound to be more
favorable than in the US.

▲ *Always* carry traveler's checks rather than cash (and, for
safety's sake, record their numbers in *two* different
places, separate from the checks). Change them at
banks rather than where you do your shopping—
you'll invariably save money.

▲ For an extended trip, an American Express card is
invaluable, since it allows you to cash a personal check
up to $1,000 ($200 in cash, the balance in travelers'
checks) at any American Express Travel Service world
wide. Call American Express for their *Traveler's Compan-
ion,* a small booklet with addresses and telephone numbers of their offices in the US and abroad.

▲ Watch the banks' posted rates of exchange, and change
a bit more money than you immediately need when
things are favorable. But don't overdo it: If you're
caught with money you have to change back by the
time you leave, you could lose money on the deal.

▲ Remember: Duty-free buying *doesn't* mean you won't

have to pay duty if these purchases push you over the allowance. Ask your travel agent about the limits before you go.

▲ Any valuables you already own (watches, jewelry, furs) may be questioned by customs on your return. To avoid any arguments, you can take them to a US Customs office before you leave to get certificates of registration of ownership. Otherwise, try to bring some other form of proof that they're yours: sales receipt, insurance policy form, certificate of appraisal.

Before you go: Send a postcard with your name and address to "Travelers' Tips," US Department of Agriculture-APHIS, Washington DC 20250. This booklet tells you what you need to know about bringing back food, animals, and plants from other countries.

Tip: Three indispensables for a trip abroad are foreign phrase books (if you don't know the language; look for American Express International Traveler's Pocket Dictionary and Phrase Books, published by Simon & Schuster); a pocket calculator (for figuring prices correctly and quickly); and an absolute *minimum* of ten extra passport-size photos of yourself. You'll need replacement photos if you lose your passport. Also, certain visas require several pictures, and you never know when you might change your mind and add another country to your itinerary! *Bon Voyage!*

7 Smooth Sailing: More Travel Tips

*H*ere are some extra tips to help insure that your trip, wherever you go, is smooth, fun, and safe.

HEALTH AND FITNESS

▲ Dare we say it? Think ahead to what time of the month it will be for you while you're away. Tampons and sanitary napkins are always cheaper in the big boxes— the bulky kind you don't want to buy on a trip. Bring what you'll need. This is especially important if you're going abroad, where your regular brand can be phenomenally expensive or impossible to find.

▲ Vacation time is not the time to go on a diet. Your

system has enough to do just trying to regulate itself under stressful conditions. Since so many of your meals are eaten out, however, it's a good idea to keep at least one meal, preferably lunch, a bit light. You can buy an inexpensive Styrofoam ice chest at a variety store when you arrive, fill it with ice (in a plastic bag), and stock it with fruit juice, cheese, and fruit. It'll be easy to pick and choose from your stock and put together a lunch that can go in your handbag.

▲ If you're on a regular program of exercise at home, do plan to keep it up while away. Bring your running shoes; they're worth the weight. If you lift weights, though, you might just have to switch to swimming or other exercise. Although there are lots of so-called travel weights on the market, they still tend to be bulky and heavy. The best idea: Bring a jump rope. You can use it in your room whenever you like, and it's light!

▲ Don't overlook local or cable exercise programs on the hotel TV—they can be the perfect way to start off the morning with a burst of energy.

MORE LIKE HOME . . .

▲ When you pack, drop a sachet or scented card (like the ones that come with department store bills) into your bag for a lightly (and lusciously) scented wardrobe.

▲ If you're a nest-oriented type who's prone to homesickness, bring a photo or two of your loved one(s) to place on the hotel dresser. Just make sure the frame isn't glass—choose a flat Plexiglas one.

▲ If you like your coffee or tea in the morning before leaving your room, avoid high room-service charges by bringing a plastic mug, heating coil (available in travel shops), and tea bags or a bag of instant coffee along with you. Packets or cubes of bouillon or broth are great, too, for afternoon pick-me-ups.

▲ A roll of Scotch tape is a lightweight version of a lint remover: Just wrap a strip of tape a few times around your fingers, sticky side out.

SMOOTH AND SAFE

▲ Make sure you always have at least five dollars in one-dollar bills (or the equivalent in local currency) in your pocket for easy tipping.

▲ Always try to have a bellhop accompany you to your room when you first arrive: It's safer, and it saves hassle if the room is untidy or unsatisfactory (you'll have a witness).

▲ How many times have you left a vacation spot with your room key in your pocket? So have a lot of other people—meaning that at a given time ten or twenty other people may also have a key to your room. The moral: Avoid bringing valuables, but if you must do so, check them in the hotel safety deposit box.

▲ If your room is burglarized, don't hesitate to report it. Just be sure to get a copy of the police report, without which you can't make an insurance claim.

▲ When you're in your room, it's a good idea to keep the deadbolt or safety chain locked. Ditto windows and sliding doors.

▲ When you leave your room, do as you would at home: Leave on a light, and/or the TV (with the volume fairly low).

▲ Make sure your insurance policies are in order before you leave; talk to a travel agent about his/her recommendations for things you aren't already covered for.

▲ It's wise to get trip-cancellation insurance if you're going on a package tour or taking a charter flight. If you get sick and can't go, or if you must interrupt your trip, this may be the only way not to lose *all* the money you've already invested.

SHOPPING TIPS

▲ If you can't find the right kind of travel clothes and accessories in your area, here are a few mail-order sources to try:

• Banana Republic, 224 Grant Ave., San Francisco, CA 94108 (catalog $1; good safari-style clothes for sporty wear)

- Land's End, Dodgeville, WI 53595 (free catalog; sports clothes and soft luggage)
- L. L. Bean, Inc., Freeport, ME 04033 (free catalog; hard-wearing sports clothes and luggage)
- Lillian Vernon, 510 South Fulton Avenue, Mount Vernon, NY 10550 (free catalog; among other things, many specialty items for travel)

▲ And while you're shopping abroad, here are just a few special bargains you shouldn't miss:

England: cashmere and other woolens; china; leather; tea
Spain: saffron; leather
Italy: gold jewelry; fine leather goods
Switzerland: watches
Japan: fresh-water pearls; ceramics and pottery
Greece: hand-tooled copper; cotton clothes
Portugal: hand-decorated faience ware
Mexico: straw hats; hammocks; rugs; cotton clothes
Thailand: silk; semiprecious stones; gold
Burma: lacquerware; jade
India: silk and cotton clothes; bone, ivory, silver, and gold (22 karat) jewelry; folk art; rugs
Nepal: woolen sweaters, blankets, shawls, rugs; carved jewelry
Singapore: *the* place for electronic equipment
Israel: antiques (Unlike most countries, here it's legal to buy and export antiquities.)

8 Annotated Checklists

EVERYTHING YOU'LL NEED, AND MORE

*I*n this chapter, I've gone a bit overboard: The following annotated lists contain *all* the extras you'd ever need to bring on a basic trip. It's up to you to do the selection—if you brought everything, you'd hardly be traveling light. Read the accompanying comments to help you decide what you'll need. Then make up your own list, tape it to the bedroom mirror, and actually mark off items as they go into your bag. Just *thinking* about something doesn't mean you'll remember to bring it!

THE NECESSITIES

Personal care. *Almost* everything on this list is essential.

▲ toothbrush. Look in travel shops or department and variety stores for a compact travel toothbrush.

▲ toothpaste

▲ dental floss. You don't need to take the whole package—just cut as many strips as you'll need.

▲ tampons/sanitary napkins. Depending on where you're going, and when and how long you'll be away, don't forget them; they can be hard to find or very expensive. Take just what you'll need.

▲ comb/brush. Folding comb/brush combos are available in travel shops and in some department stores.

▲ hair clips/pins/bands

▲ soap. Most hotel rooms have it, but if your skin is sensitive, bring your own.

▲ deodorant. Remember that a roll-on or stick takes up less room than an aerosol can.

▲ talcum powder

▲ mineral water spray. A small can is a pure luxury, but one that can be worth its weight for spritzing on your face to feel refreshed, especially in a hot climate.

▲ clippers/nail file

▲ shower cap

▲ packet soap (for hand-washables)

▲ liquid neutral shoe polish (in a squeeze bottle)

▲ sewing kit (including safety pins and extra buttons)

▲ spot remover pads or pencil

▲ cotton swabs

▲ Scotch tape (to use as a lint remover)

▲ moist towelettes (in individual packets)

▲ small plastic bags (for wet or soiled clothes, and shoes)

Beauty products.

▲ makeup (day/night combos). Remember what I told you in the opening chapter about paring down your makeup needs.

▲ razor and blades. Think about bringing disposable razors—they're usually good for about four uses, and they're lightweight and inexpensive.

▲ moisturizer. For this and similar items, remove excess packaging, and transfer contents from large or breakable containers to smaller plastic bottles and jars. Many of these items, however, are available in trial or travel sizes.

▲ shampoo

▲ creme rinse/conditioner

▲ sunscreen/tanning lotion

▲ lip balm. This is especially important on sporting trips, as is some form of moisturizer.

▲ nail polish and remover. Look for the pre-soaked pads of remover; they're much more portable than a bottle and cotton balls.

Medications.

▲ prescription drugs. Be certain to bring ample amounts, as well as copies of the prescriptions.

▲ Lomotil or similar. A good thing to ask your doctor about, especially if you're going abroad.

▲ Pepto-Bismol/Alka-Seltzer

▲ aspirin

▲ hydrocortisone cream. An excellent thing to have on hand for rashes, bites, and burns that might develop on a camping trip, or abroad.

▲ corn/bunion pads; moleskin

▲ extra pair of glasses/contacts. And don't forget the prescription.

▲ contact lens solutions/saline tablets (and any other lens-cleaning essentials)

▲ Visine or similar

▲ multivitamins. These can be a great help to your body when you're traveling and most likely to ignore the needs that a well-balanced diet would satisfy.

▲ adhesive bandages

▲ insect repellent. Creams and lotions are generally easier to carry than aerosols, and are just as effective.

Tools and Small Appliances.

▲ Swiss Army knife. A great little invention. An especially useful one combines a corkscrew, knife, tweezers, can opener, and manicure scissors. You'll be equipped for an impromptu picnic any time.

▲ pocket mirror

▲ hair dryer. Think twice about bringing one, unless you absolutely rely on it. If you do need to bring one, there are a number of small-but-powerful dryers on the market, some of which come ready for traveling with voltage adapters (like the Krups Type 451). Leave the bulky traveling case at home.

▲ travel alarm clock

▲ collapsible umbrella. And if you'll be in wet climes, don't forget the folding rain hat and/or rubbers.

▲ elastic clothesline. Found in most department stores' notions or travel sections, it's a great little item that doesn't take up much space. You can wash out lingerie and other small items and hang them to dry in your hotel room, and thereby avoid having to bring the entire contents of your underwear drawer.

▲ inflatable hangers. These are a must if you plan to wash out delicate blouses and sweaters.

▲ manicure set. Bring one if you rely on it—or if you don't bring a Swiss Army knife.

▲ travel iron. One of those items some travelers swear by, and others find a nuisance. Most large hotels in the US have overnight dry cleaning services, but they can be expensive. On a business trip where you're not certain of what's available, you might prefer to bring the iron and be sure of wrinkle-free clothes.

▲ bottle opener/can opener/corkscrew. If you still persist in not getting a Swiss Army knife!

FOR TRIPS ABROAD

In addition to the above . . .

▲ pocket calculator. For figuring currency exchange.
▲ washcloth. Some of the things you count on finding in hotels are simply not provided abroad.
▲ rubber sink-stopper. You may not find one of these in your bathroom, and they're crucial to hand-wash clothes.
▲ liquid soap. Even soap may be missing; besides, a tube of liquid soap can travel more easily than a wet bar.
▲ electric plug adapters. This is a necessity if you bring any electrical appliances.
▲ paper tissues. Some small packets of these can be a great help in some of the more out of the way spots (and many Mediterranean and Asian countries) where toilet paper is hard to come by.
▲ flashlight and batteries. A good idea if you're going anywhere other than western Europe. Most department stores stock inexpensive (and *small*) disposable flashlights—perfect for traveling!

THE FUN EXTRAS

If you've got the room and the special interest, trips provide the perfect opportunity to indulge yourself a bit.

▲ Tiger balm. Available in Oriental and health food stores in little tins, this is a little like a powerful Ben-Gay, and can be used to rub away muscle soreness. A little applied to your temples can get rid of a headache, sometimes faster than aspirin.

▲ earplugs/eyeshades. These can be wonderfully useful in helping you to get shut-eye on public transportation, and even in noisy or light-filled hotel rooms.

▲ 100-watt light bulb (for US travel). Many times, to keep electric bills down, hotels use low-watt bulbs. If you're addicted to reading in bed, your own light bulb will help. Just be sure to pack it carefully, in its own package, or wrap it in tissue paper and place it in a shoe (but not in checked-through luggage!).

▲ tea bags/instant coffee/bouillon/electric heating coil/ plastic mug. If you like a hot beverage first thing in the morning, make your own and avoid high-cost room service. You can buy a folding plastic cup (camping supply stores have them) if you want to save space.

▲ night-light. It can be a comfort in an unfamiliar room.

▲ portable tape player and tapes. A "personal stereo" and some favorite tapes can also be a comfort. And on public transportation, you won't bother anyone else if you want to listen.

▲ jump rope. Easily packable, it provides great exercise, even in your room.

▲ bath salts or beads. Fill a plastic bag with your favorite bath preparation, so you can enjoy the same relaxation away as you do at home.

▲ votive candle. Always a nice touch in a dreary hotel room and especially handy when traveling off the beaten track where electricity is sporadic or nonexistent.

A FINAL SEND-OFF

Remember how before a trip you used to say, with great dismay (and just a touch of fear) in your voice, "I guess I'd better go pack now"? That feeling was a product of a fear of the unknown. You always knew that forewarned was forearmed, but now finally you know how to apply that knowledge to travel. There's no reason not to feel confident—and joyful—about getting ready for a trip. The confidence of knowing how to prepare is your ticket to traveling light and getting there in style.

The main thing I hope you've gotten from reading this book is just how possible it is to command your own destiny. Since that doesn't come easy at first, though, you do have to take the time to see, for instance, that the wardrobe pieces you've selected work well for your sense of style, for your body, and for the particular trip you're taking. After that, it can be a coast downhill.

Practice makes perfect. Soon, I think, you'll be able to call yourself the world-class traveler that every one of us can be. You *can* travel without worries—just try it and see! Here's to your success!